THE
DIVINE WISDOM
OF
INDIAN RISHIS

THE

DIVINE WISDOM

OF

INDIAN RISHIS

OR

AN ESSENCE

OF THE

HIDDEN VEDIC TRUTHS & YOGA PHILOSOPHY

BY

SWAMI SHIVGAN CHAND.

GYAN

Published by

GYAN

Gyan Publishing House
5, Ansari Road
Daryaganj, New Delhi-110002
Phone: 011-47034999, 9811692060
E-mail: books@gyanbooks.com

Distribution Network
gyanbooks.com
India, USA, Canada, UK, Australia

ISBN: 978-93-6280-072-5 (HB)
First Published, 1899

2nd Impression 2024

Printed at: Gyan Press, Delhi.

THE DIVINE WISDOM OF INDIAN RISHIS
Author: SWAMI SHIVGAN CHAND

THE

DIVINE WISDOM

OF

INDIAN RISHIS

OR

AN ESSENCE

OF THE

HIDDEN VEDIC TRUTHS & YOGA PHILOSOPHY.

(Comprising a summary of the *Darshanas*, i. e., the *Yoga*, *Sankhya*, *Nyaya*, *Vaisheshika*, *Mimansa*, & *Vedanta* Philosophies; *with other valuable information*; originally written for the *World's Religious Parliament*, which has favorably mentioned it in its report at page 1558.)

BY

SWAMI SHIVGAN CHAND.

Agra:
PRINTED AT THE MOON PRESS.
1899.

PREFACE.

(By Munshi Gopi Nath, Deputy Magistrate, Kekri and Secretary, 6th Kayastha Conference, Rajputana).

The world is transient and so are all the things which belong to it. Impressed with this idea, our ancient Rishis have always preferred the *eternal bliss* to the *worldly bliss.* Necessarily therefore they had to resort to the *yoga* practices, without which the desired goal cannot be attained.

To give a succint idea of the *yoga* philosophy and of the other *shastras* generally has been the sole object of the author, the well known Kayastha reformer Swami Shivgan Chandji.

Swamiji's name is not only familar in and respected by the Kayastha community, but also by many other public bodies in India. His *charming, extempore* lectures on various subjects, always full of enthusiasm and original thoughts, ornamented by Sanscrit Shlokas and Arabic proverbs, by Persian couplets and English phrases, delivered in a frank and bold, but easy and pathetic style, probing the hearts of the hearers, will never be forgotten by those who have once heard them. It was these lectures and the *exemplary life of the lecturer* that aroused the sleeping masses in the Kayastha Community.

When Swamiji expressed his intention, 4 years ago, to lead a passive life and break his *active connection* with the social Refrom work, a very deep regret was felt by the Public and especially the Kayasthas. They will now be glad to know that even in his *passive life* Swamiji has worked much more than many lip-reformers. In fact having dived into the ocean of Immensity and interviewed with the sages of antiquity there, Swamiji has brought for us drops of the waters of Immortality. For his letter with its supplement, fully deserving the name "DIVINE WISDOM OF INDIAN RISHIS" is not only replete with philosophic matter for thoughtful readers, but also contains hidden *divine truths* so clearly unfolded as to satisfy the spiritual hunger and thirst of truth seekers.

The pamphlet was originally written with a view to represent the Divine Wisdom of our Rishis, at the worlds' religious parliament at Chicago. The Vedic religion of the Hindus is noted for its antiquity; to proclaim its eminence and extend its usefulness to the whole world is the chief object of this pamphlet.

Certainly one cannot do justice to a serious subject like religion within the narrow compass of a pamphlet like this, but to treat a subject of such grave character in so plain and characteristic a language, is more than ordinary human work. The greatest possible amount of thought has been expressed in the fewest and clearest words.

Technicalities which are generally great stumbling blocks in the way of readers have been as far as possible avoided, or explained in a clear manner. The remarks preceding the yoga philosophy deserve special attention. A brief history of various Hindu sects with their principles seems to have been embodied, with a view to enable the reader, to compare their religious truths and principles placed side by side and thus to decide which particular sect one should like the best; but this task is beset with difficulties innumerable and unsurmountable. To make a choice of one particular system, out of the so many, attends a preliminary conviction of that faith. The best use the reader can make of this pamphlet, is to glean the subtle truths underlying each system, and then try to find out a focus, wherein those truths can be centred, and thus to prepare a religious force for setting in motion a true universal religion for the whole world.

Why there are discrepancies in religious principles, is to be accounted for by the fact that by a constant use of any particular form of religion, one contracts a firm attachment to it. The fornalities of religion and the preliminaries in certain ceremonies do gradually become a part and parcel of religion which they do not at all deserve. The object of a true religion ought to be to accept all truths as truths, and to regard their adjuncts and compendiums as such only and not as truths themselves. *Truth* requires no advocate, no help; for it is a self-shining substance in itself; but it is the darkness of our inward mirror which obstructs the reflections of the rays of truth. It is better to purify this inward mirror, by a practical life of piety, abstinence and a systematic practice of the yoga. One would himself feel improved by these practices, by an experience of a few years, and the one great good he will attain, is the substantial power of original thinking. If India lacks any thing at present, it is the originality of thought, and the power of original conception. It is a great charge that is brought home to India, the mother of the religions of the world.

The following are the remarks from one of the ablest sons of India"* * * The Indian intellect has been dormant for centuries; original thought disappeared with the old Rishis, the fermentation of religious and philosophic ideas ceased with the decline of Buddhism, philosophy became verbose and wasted itself in trifling subteli ties, poetry assumed an artificial character, religion degenerated into forms, ceremonies and superstitions, and custom became a hideous tyrant, * * * * and the task and heavy responsibility of regenerating her (India) has devolved upon ourselves, who have felt the influence of thought on every subject that has an interest for humanity. It must be stipulated that literature and philosophy have a fresh start, our vernaculars must be improved, and the desire for knowledge be propagated. The great inequities and falsehoods of our soical institutions and customs must be corrected, the standard of practical morality raised, tastes improved, higher ideas placed before the people, and religion purified and reformed."

I dare say that the select thoughts and principles, arguments and facts, embodied in this pamphlet, will well satisfy our aforementioned esteemed brother as well as other thoughtful well-wishers of India.

It is a pride for India and especially for our community that Swamiji has explained the hidden Divine Wisdom of the old Rishis.

Although Swamiji wrote his letter for the religious parliament, yet he has thought it advisable not to refuse the over-whelming requests of his many friends to publish it, and circulate it as a religious tract for the religious world and the seekers of truth.

It is hoped the pamphlet would be found well-adapted to the purpose for which it is intended, and that it will not fail in achieving the required object before long.

The exposition of abstruse subjects and illumination of truth is by no means an easy task, and had it not been for the extraordinary gift, the author has acquired, by the practice of yoga, such a work in its present form would have been an impossibility.

As an encouragement for the advance of religion, the pecuniary charges incurred in the publication of this pamphlet, have been very gladly borne by His Highness the MAHARAJA DHIRAJ SRI NAHAR SINGHJI, the Chief of SHAHPURA State in RAJPUTANA. The Maharaja is one of the most *refined* and *generous* princes of India. He has also a special taste for religion and is the *head* of a constitutional Society of the Vedic Religion.

Dated Kekri, 5th March 1894.

G. N.

ओ३म्

To

THE SECRETARY,

World's Religious Parliament,

CHICAGO.

DEAR SIR,

Before venturing to lay down the following for your and the religious Congress favourable consideration, I beg to inform you of the circumstances under which I have thought it advisable to write this letter.

I am a native of India—Punjab Province: having been brought up in a good family* and received general education, I was at a very early age appointed to a lucrative post in the Government service, but from my boyhood I had a special taste for religion; and having got the position of an Inspecting Officer I had opportunities of visiting almost all big places in the Punjab, and wherever I heard of a good Sadhu (one devoted to God) I used to go to him in the odds and ends of my time and talk with him on *Religion.* Thus my information about Religion became wide, but the more I drank from the religious spring, the more I felt myself thirsty for it, and at last the saying that "One man cannot serve two masters" haunted my spirit. I prayed God to take me solely in His service and to my great joy the prayers were accepted.

I resigned the service in the beginning of 1886, and spent one full year in calm meditation under the supervision of my *Spiritual Guide,* who is a great Yogi, but like Zeno, has, of all the virtues, chosen that of silence. He is now about eighty years old and is said not to have spoken a single word for about twenty years.

---

* The late lamented Kunjbehari Lal, Prime Minister, Alwar State in Rajputana was Swamiji's nephew; and our much esteemed brother Munshi Bhim Sen, Pleader, President, Kayastha Provincial Sabha Punjab is Swamiji's very near relation.

After one year's calm meditation and at my guide's indirect suggestion and at the pressing request of some leading Kayasthas I devoted myself to the Social and Intellectual Reform of the Kayastha Community. This community is very prominent in India, it numbers about 2,200,000 souls and is scattered all over India. I also have the honour to belong to this time-honoured community. I worked there with all my heart and soul making a lecturing tour through almost all the four quarters of India *i. e.*, Bengal, Madras, Bombay, Rajputana, the Central Provinces, the N.-W. Provinces, Oudh and the Punjab, and delivering hundreds of lectures the result of which was the establishment of about 300 societies. I also compiled a number of useful books and pamphlets for them which go under the name of "The Social Reform Series."* The

* Of the numerous books compiled by Swamiji, many have appeared without the author's name. Those well known to the Kayastha public are as follows :—

(1.) Rafiq-i-Tiflan or "companion of the children." This pamphlet points out the many pitfalls to which boys of immature age are exposed in their juvenile career. The dialogue between the Moulvi and the Pandit is very amusing, and the lecture of the Sadhu is highly instructive and brimful of advice not only to boys but to young men generally.

(2.) Rafiq-i-Noujawanan or "companion for the youth." This pamphlet is indispensable for the guidance of the youth when emerging from their School or College career. It points out the many temptations which beset them in the path of life and shows how they should avoid them. The stories of Ikbal Singh Head Master and of Chuha Ram Clerk are very original and full of interest and warning. It was very favourably reviewed by the many eminent critics to whose scrutiny it was subjected. Mr. J. C. Nesfield, M. A. (Director of Public Instruction, N. W. P.) was so much impressed with the value of the book that he issued a circular and a very large number of the book has been purchased by his Department for presentation in prizes.

(3.) Rafiq-i-Piran or "companion to the aged." It is a very interesting little brochure showing in the form of a dialogue how the older generation is disposed towards the Reform movement, and pointing out the good which the retired officials and those who had sufficient time and means at their command are capable of doing to the younger generation. At the end very good pieces of advice in the form of religious extracts from Gita are given in a very stirring and pathetic language. This pamphlet is under the Press.

Kayasthas have a very good and complete organisation ; to keep a watch over the local sabhas and give them every possible help, 13 Provincial Sabhas have been formed through the Election System : they have also one Head-Sabha for the whole of India, which consists of the cream of their society and its Secretary is our most

(4.) Sandhia Paddhiti or "Prayer Book." It has been very favorably received by the Kayastha Community as well as by the general public. It was designed in consultation with many men with a view to facititate the performance of religious ordinances twice a day, *i.e.*, every morning and evening, according to Vedic religion and has met with exceptional success. It contains many selected *mantras* from the Vedas together with their translation in easy Hindi and Urdu, and also full explanations are given where necessary. No less an authority than Babu Ram Saran Dass, M. A., the eminent Sanscrit Scholar of the Kayastha Community and fellow of the Allahabad University and Member of the Asiatic Society pronounces the book to be free from all sectarian bias, and gives full credit for the successful execution of a task which was by no means easy in its character. These pamphlets go under the name of "Social Reform Series" and were compiled by Swamiji at the special request of certain persons and were edited by the late lamented Professor Nand Kumar, B. A. and Pandit Kirpa Shunkra, M. A. of Agra.

(5.) Toufah-tul-Mulazmin or a "Present to Public Servants." This book was compiled by Swamiji at the request of the Kayastha Literary Association of Allahabad and has undergone two editions under the auspices of that association. It contains most useful and practical advice for the officials. Briefly speaking it enumerates the qualifications necessary for an official and suggests how to acquire them ; how to respect and obey the superiors, and treat with love the equals and the subordinates, &c., &c. The book has been very well received by both the Kayastha Community and the general public and has been patronized by many Heads of Departments and Educational Officers.

(6.) A-i-nah-i-Rasti or "The Mirror of Truth." Swamiji wrote it at the very pressing request of some membecs of the Aryan Debating Club of Gujranwala in the Punjab. It has won a prize for Rs. 50 together with the cost of publication of 500 copies, in an open competition, held under the supervision of an efficient committee appointed by the Sat Sabha, of Baleli in Biluchistan. The vice of telling lies and the virtues of truthfulness are very well portrayed by stirring historical examples. Also a comparison is made of the thoughts of eminent Europeans and Asiatics about truthfulness, and some practical hints given to achieve this noble quality. This pamphlet or rather prize essay has been patronized by Educational Department and undergone many editions.

popular, most beloved, and most energetic brother, Mr. Lakshmi Narain, Barrister-at-law who by this time must be enjoying the pleasure of your company, and must have personally explained to you about the Kayastha Social Reform.

After about 3 years I was directed by my Spiritual Guide to sever my connection from the above work and to keep myself as far as possible aloof from all the external influences and devote the whole of my attention to the practice of Yoga, a most sacred and secret science by which the inner mechanism of body and soul is studied.

7. **Sant-i-mat Catechism** or "Religious beliefs of Guru Nanak, the saviour of the Punjab; Daduji, the once eminent leader of religious thoughts in Rajputana; of Kabir Bhagat, the mysterious weaver and religious leader of Kashi (Benares); of Radha Swami, the Guru and Spiritual Guide of Rai Salig Ram Bahadur are explained in this pamphlet in the form of questions and answers. Swamiji wrote this pamphlet at the desire of Rai Salig Ram Bahadur, a Mathur Kayastha and a retired Post Master General, now leading a new religious sect called "Radha Swami." The Rai Sahib published this pamphlet for the benefit of his sect and the public at large. The Rai Sahib and the doctrines of his sect have been very favorably spoken of in the pamphlet.

8. **Mumukshu Mitra** or "A Guide to Seekers after Salvation." It gives a short description of Yoga Philosophy; the conditions to be fulfilled by a Yoga student; the benefit to be derived from a regular practice of Yoga and the method to practise Huta Yoga and Raj Yoga are given in this nice little pamphlet

9. Gyan Dipka or "**Lamp** of (religious) Knowledge." Swamiji wrote it at the request of Diwan Bhagat Bihari Lal, Judge in the Jeypur State. It is divided into 3 parts; the 1st contains an explanation of almost all the every day use terms of our religious books generally not understood by ordinary reader; a brief description of human body is also given from which it appears that atma or soul is pervading through the whole of the body by means of *Sukhmana nari*. The 2nd part consists of an ably written preface; and the 3rd is an epitome of the famous book Bhagvat Gita chapter by chapter. It is generally believed by many religious men of high reputation that of all the Tikas or commentaries written on Gita and which are no less than about 52 in number, none is so brief, clear, and instructive as that rendered by Swamiji.

Accordingly, I commenced practising certain Yoga Sadhans (practices) and am now leading a passive and solitary life since 1890, only appearing before the public either in emergent cases or at the Annual Meetings of the Kayasthas called "The Kayastha Conference."

It was by a strange combination of circumstances that I came to know in July 1892 of your most laudable efforts and truly philanthropic enterprise to hold a Universal Religious Congress and consider therein the general principles of all religions prevailing in the world.

Immediately I knew of it I tried my best to rouse the leading religious bodies to send their delegates to your Congress. It was my firm determination that if no delegate was sent from the Punjab, I would myself join your assembly, but the Arya Samaj, after full consideration deputed two of its members and therefore I was satisfied and postponed my coming, especially because long journeys are forbidden in Yoga practice, as they disturb the tranquility of mind, except under very emergent circumstances.

Last week, however, I learnt that the Arya Samaj failed to send its mission; at this last moment I tried to come myself, but Indian Sadhus, like myself, quite destitute of money and other comforts cannot undertake expensive journeys on such a short notice; of course, had I expressed my intention to join your Congress, a month earlier, my numerous friends and sympathisers would, have gladly and at once arranged for my expenses.

At this eleventh or rather thirteenth hour, however, according to the saying, "Something is better than nothing" I sit down to write this letter.

---

10. Apt-up-desh or "Indisputable Truth." This pamphlet is a commentary in Urdu on selected Sanscrit Shlokas from the famous Maharaja Bhartariji who abdicated his throne to lead a hermit life. It is divided into 3 parts. The 1st contains certain laws of morality for children and youngmen and is called Niti Shatak. The 2nd contains the laws of leading a peaceful and happy family life, and is called Shrangar Shatak and is intended for the youth. The 3rd

I must tell you here that our much advanced and esteemed religious men of the old school are so much convinced of the *nothingness* of this changeful and perishable world and are so much absorbed in the improvement of their inner-self that they do not like or care to spare even one single moment for any worldly affair, however grand it may be.

There is, however, another class of religious people generally known as the outcome of the British Rule and English Education and influence. This class, though yet in infancy, is divided into many divisions and sub-divisions, the more important of which are the Bramho Samaj, the Arya Samaj, the Theosophical Society, and the Sanatan Dharma Sabha.

The Bramho Samaj was founded by a very patriotic and enthusiastic spirit Raja Ram Mohan Rai about the middle of the current century. This Samaj is more popular in Calcutta and its neighbourhood, though its influence was once felt throughout the whole of India, and it is still working quietly in many cities and towns. Mahrishi Divindra Nath Tagore and Babu Keshub Chandra Sen and some other personages have worked and many are working still very zealously and successfully for this Samaj.†

impresses the instability of this changeful world and is intended for the aged men and is called Vairag Shatak. The book is full of most useful and practical advice alike for men, women, old or young.

† The following are the Principles of Brahmo Dharma :—

1. There is only one God, who is the Creator, Preserver, and Saviour of the world. He is a spirit, infinite in wisdom, love, justice, and holiness; omnipotent, eternal and blissful.

2. The human soul is immortal, and capable of infinite progress, and is responsible to God for its doings.

3. God must be worshipped in spirit and truth. Divine worship is necessary for attaining true felicity and salvation.

4. Love to God, and carrying out His will in all the concerns of life, constitute true worship.

After about two dozens of years since the establishment of the Bramho Samaj, a very learned and energetic Sanyasi Sawami Daya Nanda Suraswati well-versed in the Vedas commenced the religious reformation of our country. He tried in the first instance to establish Sanscrit schools and teach the Brahmins their true Dharma or religion: but having given up this mission he made a lecturing tour and held religious discussions wherever his opponents wished to do so, and was always victorious. Hindus, Mohamedans and Christians all came to discuss the religious theories but could not stand before his powerful oratory and weighty arguments Swamiji established Arya Samajes in many important places such as Bombay, Lahore &c., many of the ruling chiefs of Rajputana and the big land holders and true well-wishers of India showed their full sympathy with him. After less than a dozen of year's work Swamiji died, some say having been poisoned by his adversaries. His unexpected death, though a great loss, gave a real impetus to the hearts of many a true Arya, who established in commemoration of his death a College at Lahore (called Daya Nand Anglo-Vedic College) and an Ashram (an abode for learned hermits) and a school at Ajmere. They have also established two orphanages and many female schools. The Arya Samajes are more popular in the Punjab, N.-W. Provinces and Rajputana, although their truths are being discussed and accepted in almost all the nooks and corners of India.

5. Prayer and dependence on God, and a constant realization of His presence are the means of attaining spiritual strength.

6. No created object is to be worshipped as God, nor any person or book to be considered as infallible, and the sole means of salvation.

7. The Fatherhood of God and Brotherhood of man.

8. God rewards virtue, and punishes sin. His punishments are remedial and not eternal.

9. Cessation from sin, accompanied by sincere repentance, is the only atonement for it; and union with God in wisdom, goodness, and holiness a true salvation.

These Samajes hold weekly meetings on Sundays, the majority the Aryas being law practitioners or Government servants. In ie opening they offer prayers, then a text or two are read from the Vedas or other religious books in the form of a Sermon, after which one or more lectures are delivered and at each interval *bhajans* (or religious songs) are sung with music. A special peculiarity in these Samajes is that they hold Annual Meetings in which all the leading members from far and near meet together and discuss all the leading questions personally, and collect large sums of money for different charitable purposes. *

* The following are the principles of the Arya Samaj.—

1.—God is the Fountain of all true knowledge, and the primeval cause of all things knowable.

2.—Worship is alone due to God who is All-truth, All-knowledge, All-beatitude Incorporeal, Almighty, Just, Merciful, Unbegotten, Infinite Unchangeable without a beginning, Incomparable, the support and the Lord of all, All-pervading, Omniscient, Imperishable, Immortal, exempt from fear, Eternal, Holy and the cause of the universe.

3.—The Vedas are the books of true knowledge, and it is the pa mount duty of every Arya to read or hear them read, to teach and p ch them to others.

4.—An Arya should always be ready to accept truth and renounce untruth when discovered.

5.—Truth arrived, after consummate deliberation should be his guiding principle in all actions.

6.—The primary object of the Samaj is to do good to the world by improving the physical, intellectual, spiritual, moral and social condition of mankind.

7.—Due love for all and appreciation of justice, an Arya should manifest in his behavour towards others.

8.—He should endeavour to defuse knowledge and dispel ignorance.

9.—He should not be content with his own improvement but look for it in that of others.

10.—In matters which affect the general social well-being of our race he ought to discard all differences and not allow his individuality to interfere but in strictly personal matters every one may have his own way.

In Swami Dayanand's time an American gentleman Colonel Olcott and a lady by name Madam Bladvasky opened correspondence with Swamiji, and invited him to America; but on his declining the invitation owing to press of work in India, they themselves came over to India and paid many visits to Swamiji. For some time, they were on very good terms. The Colonel and the Madam started an English paper—The Theosophist—in which Swamiji was always eulogised, but afterwards some difference of opinion intervened. The Colonel and the Madam made lecturing tours and began to establish Theosophical Societies all over India. The English knowing Indians generally showed sympathy with them. They fixed the Head Quarters of their parent Society first at Bombay and subsequently removed it to Madras. They are more popular in that Presidency now. The Indians are generally of opinion that this society is more inclined towards Buddhism. They also think that the founders are more in touch with Foreign countries such as Thibet, Ceylon, China, Japan, America, &c.; and although there is a large number of their branch societies in India, yet many of them are merely nominal.

The Theosophical Society has rendered very good services to our country especially in trying to revive Sanscrit and translating many old Sanscrit works into English. But the prominence given to ghost phenomena and miracles by them wants the test of time before ready and general acceptance.*

The Sanatan Dharma Sabha has been started, it is believed, by some Pundits of the old fashion to check the progress of the Arya Samaj. This Sabha seems to be in touch with the uneducated masses and the general public,

---

* PRINCIPLES OF THEOSOPHY.

1. To form the members of a Universal brother-hood of Humanity without distinction of race, creed, sex, caste or colour

2. To promote the study of the Aryan and other Eastern Literatures, religious philosophies and sciences, to demonstrate their importance to humanity.

3. A third object pursued by a portion only of the members of the society is to investigate unexplained laws of nature and the physical powers of man.

though many learned and able men are also supporting it. The chief difference between the Arya Samaj and the Sanatan Dharma Sabha is that the former denounces *idol worship*, while the latter enjoins it, in other respects they have little or no *important* difference. Many thinking men are of opinion that a time is near at hand when these two most important and leading bodies will be amalgamated: I also pray God that such a time may come soon, nay, my prayers are that all human beings may profess one religion, or at least all men believing in one true God may adopt one religious code (and that code cannot be any other than the *Laws of Nature*) for their guidance. As this can only be done by the help and co-operation of a large number of wise, thinking and learned men, it is my firm belief that my dream can only be realised in an assemblage like yours.

Believers in God have, no doubt, very different and strange ideas about God, *i. e.* to say each individual and each congregation according to their faculties of reason and belief display the like image of God and have moreover *Mediators* between themselves and their God, and thus instead of worshipping the true God, they fall a victim to numerous kinds of superstition and idolatory, so much so that sometimes they do not, even, hesitate to molest or kill other living beings under the pretence of religion, or under the belief that their mediator will save them from God's punishment for their bad deeds. In this and many other respects our Vedic religion, I dare say, has an undisputed superiority over them. In fact our sacred Vedas reveal the laws of nature and enjoin on all human beings to worship *Nature's God.* There is no mediator recommended, nor can any man's thoughts, sayings and doings (good or bad) escape the notice of the Almighty God whose justice is impartial.

The word Veda is derived from (विद्) *Vid*, which means to know, to think or to see; and Veda literally means '*Fountain of knowledge.*' God revealed the Vedas to certain most pious and pure minded Rishis and *can* and *will* reveal them to each and every person who would practise Yoga (and be the right focus for the contralisation of Divine-light) and attain that stage of piety and purity which the above Rishis in the beginning of creation did.

The most Scientific Philosophy of Karma (good or bad deed, thought or utterance); of man's option and free will to do Karma and the inevitable necessity of his receiving the fruit of his Karmas at the hands of Providence; of the immortality and transmigration of soul; of the omni-science and omni-presence of God, and above all of the way by which to approach God are very beautifully and clearly given in our Vedas and Khat-Darshanas (the Six Schools of Philosophy)† and other Sat Shastras (true religious books). I regret that the shortness of time and the scope of this manuscript letter (which I am writing in the greatest hurry for the time of posting overland letters is nearly up) do not allow me to dwell on each of the above points. I cannot, however, refrain from giving you a little idea about the last point, *i. e.*, how to attain God, who dwells in the most blissful region called by our Shastras (तुर्या अवस्था) Turiya Avastha. In doing so, I shall also try to touch though briefly and in an indirect manner some of "the ten questions" which were once, long ago, published in different newspapers of India, as the questions to be considered in your Congress. The more a man is free from the anxieties and impurities of this wakeful state *Jagrat Avastha* and makes researches in his innerself, the nearer is he to the above blissful region.

There are so many laws regulating this material world that in the short life of one hundred years or so no man can know them all.* On the other hand the more he tries to know them, the more he finds his wisdom dumb and the laws too numerous and difficult to understand. For instance, our *Jotish Shastra* (Astronomy) tells us that there is no limit to this (स्थूल जगत) "Mighty visible universe." Our planet earth, though very big, is nothing in comparison with the sun, while the sun is much smaller in comparison

---

† Swamiji has been pleased to write a summary of the Darshanas which is published as a supplement of this letter.

* Truly has said a philosopher that "Art is long, Life is short."

with the whole solar system ; and there are systems above systems without number. God, though pervading through all these systems, cannot be traced there. But man is a macracosm of the whole universe ; and as the sun, though shining over every thing, is only reflected in transparent substances such as water, &c., so God's light renders itself visible only in the pure and innocent soul of man (the only tabernacle of holies in nature, God-in-man is one with Man-in-God). But the soul of an ordinary man is so much involved in worldly affairs and improper dealings that it has, so to speak, created a curtain or veil of ignorance, the root of all sins, which keeps him away from all pervading and omni-present God. To remove this आवर्ण avarna (veil or curtain) our Rishi Patanjali has suggested in his Yoga Philosophy many easy but most scientific and true methods one or two of which I give below :—

॥ वितर्क विचारा नन्दसिता रूपा नुगमात्संप्रज्ञात : (१७) ॥

Sense of the Sutra :—

By वितर्क (Vitark) is meant religious study and discussions with the learned men. In this position it is very necessary to strictly adhere to the following two instructions of Patanjaliji *viz.*—

(a) मैत्री करुणा मुदितो पेक्षाणां सुख दुःख ।
पुण्या पुण्य विषयाणाम् भावनातश्चित्त प्रसादनम् ॥ सूत्र ३३, पाद १ ॥

Sense :—

He must show friendship to all those who are living peacefully ; mercy to those who are miserable ; openheartedness to those who perform good and noble acts and must remain separate from those who are wicked. This will keep equilibrium of his mind.

(b) प्रच्छर्दन विधारणा भ्यां वा प्राणस्य (सूत्र ३४, पाद १)

Sense in English :—

To make a practice of *Pranayama, i. e.*, to sit every morning in a place open to a free current of pure and fresh air and slowly inhale the breath ; then suspend it for as many seconds as one can, and then exhale it with full force. This will keep the bodily health good and will prolong life.

After attaining the first stage of *Vitark*, he enters into the second one, the विचार (act of thinking). To make improvement in his faculty of thinking, he must have full control over his two इन्द्रि: (*i. e. Eyes* and *Ears* or the *faculties of seeing and hearing*), which lead every one to worldly affairs. Patanjali says that if the ears be shut out from external sound and made to hear the internal *harmony* and the eyes be closed and made to see the inward light (at the focus of the two eyes), or in other words if the power of these two faculties be sent back to the place whence it comes, their source will be traced to a centre of light called मनस (The Organ of will—power). This state is called आनन्दा नुगत (Happy State). If the light which strengthens the *Manas* is again traced onwards, another centre of clearer light is attained which strengthens बुधी (The Organ of Intelligence). This बुधी is, as it were, the Secretary of जीवात्मा (Human Soul). This state is called the अस्मिता नुगत. It is in this state that grand religious theories and scientific truths are discovered. The thinking power of an ordinary man comes through two media मन and इन्द्रि: and thus it becomes two times weaker and obscurer than the above. It is beyond this stage that the happy region of तुर्या (Turiya) is reached and God with His innumerable attributes and powers is conceived by the help of the above बुधी :

Patanjali says :—

विशोका वा ज्योतिष्मती। सूत्र ३६, पाद १ ॥

Again :—

मूर्धा ज्योतिषि सिद्ध दर्शनम्। सूत्र ३०, पाद ३ ॥

By calm meditation and full concentration in त्रिकुटी : (where three lights meet in the forehead, between the two eye brows) and कपाल (the cro… … head … a little hole between the cerebrum and celebrum) the reflection of the ray of God's light is perceived and Siddhas are interviewed. The great sage Vyasaji, while commenting on the last of the above *Sutras* gives the following quotations from his Vedant Upanishad :—

न पातालं न च विवरं गिरिणाम् ।
नै वान्धकारं न कुक्षयो नदीनाम् नोदधी नाम् ॥
गुहा यस्यां निहितं ब्रह्म शाश्वतं ।
बुद्धि वृत्ति मवि शिष्टां कवयो वेदयं ते ॥

Sense :—

Brahm (God) is neither sitting in the antipodes, nor in the dark caves, nor on the banks of rivers or oceans. The only cave in which he resides is called by the learned men बुद्धी (The Organ of Intelligence).

A man who thus approaches God enjoys the true happiness. His is the true religion, the highest morality. Every thing in this world adds to his happiness and he is the ideal of reverence and love to every living being. Our Rishis and Rajas of yore followed the above religious observances and instructions and made heaven of earth. The chief benefit they derived from this true religion was मोक्ष (Salvation) ; but as a secondary result they became not only kings and sovereigns, but also moral governors of their subjects. Their exemplary life spread morality of the highest order among their fellow beings. All the manners and customs adopted in their time were based on the highest kind of scientific foundations, for instance the eight kinds of marriages* and

* 1. ब्रह्म विवाह in which the bride and bridegroom must be of mature age, not less than 18 and 25 years of age respectively, they both must be learned, thoroughly moral, and should marry by mutual consent. Another name for this marriage is स्वयंवर or marriage by self choice.

2. दैव विवाह or marriage according to the consent or rather discretion of the parents.

the cremation of their dead bodies, &c., are seen up to the present day. Similarly trades and professions flourished in that period in full bloom; the Brahmins were exclusively devoted to religious and intellectual improvements; their works like *Suraj-Siddhant* which is an authority in Astronomy and *Shushrat* and *Chark* which are authorities in medicine, and *Valmiki Ramayan* which is one of the best epic poems ever written, show ample proof of their highest kind of excellence reached in these respective departments of science and literature. The Kshatryas were devoted to military arts and professions, the Vaisyas to agricultural pursuits and banking affairs; while the *sudras* served the above three sects by doing all sorts of menial work. This state of tranquility and improvement which was the result of true religion, our ancient books say, lasted for thousands upon thousands of years. But "the longest days have at last an end." Our countrymen failed to discharge their duties, *i. e.*, infringed the laws of nature and the just, and impartial, and mighty hand of Providence punished them.

I must here tell you that all religious books including the Vedas themselves are dead letters, except in so far as the finer essence of religion embodied in their repository of truths infuses

---

3. **आर्ष विवाह** in which something is taken from the bridegroom.

4. **प्रजापत्य विवाह** or marriage for the sake of happiness of the couple.

5. **असुर विवाह** in which something like bribery is given to boy or girl or to both.

6. **गान्धर्व विवाह** or the union of the boy and girl without the ceremonies of the marriage and out of season, owing to some sudden excitement. As the result of courtship.

7. **राक्षस विवाह** or taking possession of the girl by force, by fight, or by any other unfair means.

8. **पैशाच विवाह** or to commit-rape when the girl is either asleep, drunk or mad.

The 1st 4 are considered good and the last 4 bad. The 2nd is most prevalent.

itself in the living human soul and manifests itself in the pious actions of man 'from well to better daily self-surpast.' Just as it happened in the case of Rishis Patanjali, Vyasa Shankara Acharya, Guru Nanak and Swami Dayanand Saraswati, who enlightened our land with religious and spiritual illumination: and it is believed by many a thinking man that under our present peaceful reign of the British Government in which every body has full freedom of thought and speech and has besides many facilities for communicating his thoughts and utterances such as the printing press, the telegraph, the post office, the railway, the ships, &c., &c., India shall again sooner or later produce the above kind of men.

It is much to be regretted that with the advance of time, while people have been professing one God, and tracing their descent from common parents, the number of religions has been daily increasing, and their mutual tendency has been not to treat men as brethern, but to make war upon men, sometimes the question arises whether more misery and bloodshed has been caused by political conflicts or religious warfares.

Divine Wisdom now and then proclaimed its teachings in different eras through chosen men; but the word was spoken, it was listened for a time, but men forgot it again. Besides such efforts were limited to certain tracts of land and their influence seldom extended beyond those tracts to the remaining world, but in the nineteenth century when distance and time were annihilated, and the ends of the world began to meet, and the social transactions between man and man made the world look like a household, wise men thought the time was come when all men and women would live as members of one and the same family in the grand domestic economy of the world and would take their code from the *laws of nature* and meet daily at the altar of Common Father, the household Deity as brothers and sisters in common worship.

The happy news of the World's Religious Parliament confirmed our prognostics and we feel sure that in the fulness of time we will, have one Catholic and universal religion. The ways of God are wonderful and "He fulfils Himself in many ways."

In ancient times the greatest congregation was at Babel, when they made a tower to reach heaven but confusion of speech and Divine Displeasure resulted; but now it seems that it has pleased God in His infinite mercy to bring the various nationalities from all nooks and corners of His creation together at Chicago, where through His choicest blessings men unknown to each other shall understand each other and *adore* one God and then depart with a brotherly feeling and in peace and good will.

America the land of the brave and free deserved this Divine mark of pleasure. We have our deepest sympathy with you and offer our heartfelt prayers for your success.

I am, &c., &c.,

Your well-wisher,

SHIVGAN.

Dated 15th August 1893.

SUPPLEMENT.

SUMMARY OF THE SIX SCHOOLS

OF

INDIAN PHILOSOPHY

CALLED THE

KHAT DARSHANAS.

The Vedas are the most sacred treasures of spiritual and moral laws revealed to the holy and pious *Yogis* or *Rishis* through *Asampargyata Yoga* or profound meditation. Vedas are also called *Shruti* because they have been heard by the *Yogis* when they closed their ears against all the external influences and made them hear the internal harmony.

Next to the *Vedas* are *Smrities* or books written by recollection, that is to say, when Rishis in different stages of Yoga, below that of *Asampargyata* discovered any religious truths, they committed them to writing in their own mode of thought and language. It is in this latter class that the Khat Darshanas generally called by the western writers, "The Six Schools of Indian Philosophy," are counted. The word Darshana means exposition and is applied to these books because they show or trace the invisible *First Great Cause* from visible substances. For a sincere *Truth Seeker* they contain plenty of instructions which if strictly carried out would lead the follower to the path of *Salvation* (*Moksha Marga*). They point out means and methods, by a careful observance of which, a sinful and vicious life can be changed into a pious and virtuous one though by slow process.

These books seem to have been written by the sages of antiquity after attaining a deep insight into the ordinary branches of knowledge, such as Ayur Veda or medicine which is divided into about a dozen branches;* Gandharva Veda or dancing and music also divided into about a dozen various forms;† Dhanur Veda or Science of War; Artha Veda or Material Arts and Sciences for the production of wealth such as Agriculture, Architecture, and others.

After acquiring so much knowledge those who aspired to become a Rishi or a Yogi used to relinquish all the outer worldly pleasures, in order to devote the whole of their time, energy, and attention to the acquisition of the *Divine Wisdom* by the practice of the most sacred science of *Yoga* and by leading a pure and most regular life of peace and piety for years and years together. They never cared for worldly wealth as their descendants do now; their bare necessities were supplied by the State Treasury or as is the custom even up to the present time, by the general public. The wealth which they longed for was *spiritual wisdom* and *not gold*, was *Divine knowledge* and *not terrestrial treasures.* They thus acquired a most clear or rather *Divine understanding*, which enabled them to unfold many a hidden law of nature. In short these books were written by most practical men when all their faculties of the body and brain, mind and soul were in *full development.* Their object in compiling them was not to gain any sort of *remuneration, fame,* or *reputation* but *simply* to record their divine experiences in brief notes or sutras for the guidance of their pupils, who used to commit the Sutras to memory and meditate upon their meaning and sense in calm and serene hours, faithfully and rigidly following all the sadhans or exercises prescribed therein. The more they practised the sadhans, the more they understood the spirit of the Darshanas and loved and valued them with all their heart, because through them they obtained a really happy life (jewan moksha). But alas! there is nothing permanent in this *transitory world.* Those times have since been changed and the doors of divine knowledge almost closed. The descendants of the Rishis though loving and respecting the books to

---

* अर्थ, क्रिया, शस्त्र, छेदन, भेदन, लेप, चिकित्सा, निदान, औषधि, पथ्य, शरीर ।

† स्वर, राग, रागणी, समय, ताल, ग्राम, तान, वादित्र, नृत्य गीत ॥

the same degree or perhaps to a greater degree, which extends to the standard of superstitious worship, do so with blind faith only. With a few *honourable exceptions* they do not take the trouble to receive proper education and to practise the many scientific sadhans embodied in the books, and therefore do not possess such clear understanding as to grasp the spirit of the Sutras. Unfortunately they believe, through utter ignorance, that the language of the religious books is divine and that the mere recitation of the *text* without understanding its meaning or sense and without leading a thoroughly pious life as enjoined therein would grant them moksha or eternal bliss, or that state in which all the pains cease to exist, and which can only be obtained by constantly obeying the laws of nature and never breaking them. In fact the degenerate sons of the Rishis not having acquired the above-mentioned branches of knowledge, nor having practised any sadhan ordained in the Darshanas, failed to understand the true meaning and spirit of the Shastras. But not possessing sufficient moral courage to let the ignorant public know this fact, they began to suppress and misinterpret the meaning and sense of many of the aphorisms according to their defective understanding, and sometimes for their own temporary and trifling personal advantages. Thus the most useful and practical side having been overlooked and spoiled, the finer essence of the once living religion of the Darshanas began gradually to disappear; remaining only in the crystalized form, concealed in the bosom of a very few *practical sadhus* just as spring fruits are kept in the seed form in autumn. The majority of the so-called learned Brahmins and Sadhus of the present day instead of performing any kinds of *tapas* or *niskam karmas* waste their time in empty talk and fruitless discussions about *theories* and *technicalities*, while the vast majority of the illiterate and ignorant having fallen victims to the external formalities have sunk in *superstition*. It is this huge system of *technicalities* and *external formalities* with *half-truths* that is most prevalent in India now, and as one of its inevitable results, has created many a new sect constantly "waging a woful waste and wicked war" against each other about very trifling matters. It is also the above external religion of half-truths and technicalities that has come to the knowledge of our *western brethren*, and by them has sometimes been subjected to very sharp *criticism* and *sweeping attacks*. A religionist has truly said that "it is far easier and far more amusing for shallow critics to point out what is absurd and ridiculous in the religion and philosophy of the ancient world than for the earnest student to discover truth and wisdom under strange disguises." Many of our English educated Indian brethren have tried to refute the charges brought against their religion by such means as seemed to them reconciliatory to the western science and philosopy; the thought perhaps not occurring to them that the *worth* and *superiority* of our religion and religious books is not because their truths and theories coincide with those of the west, but because they contain most sublime and original thoughts about morality, spirituality, and practical lessons of higher science and philosophy. "They contain the noblest morality, the purest piety, the most advanced inspiration and also treasures of science, treasures of philosophy, wrapped in pictorial language." They do not know, moreover, that by the deep study and careful practice of our religious writings, we can have a full knowledge of the innermost recesses of our body, which has so many structures within structures and functions within functions that an ordinary man can hardly keep them all constantly in full growth and proper working order; and can also know the true nature and the innumerable powers of atma or soul and its connection with the body, *i. e.*, how they both have been united and how they can be dis-united. When this connection is well understood, the body with all its passions becomes fully subdued and can be left at any time optionally, and especially at the time of death, just as a bird leaves a tree and flies away.

In short our religion and religious books like the **Darshanas** have a superiority because they teach a complete science of body and soul.

But it is not an easy task to propagate these religious truths, both because the majority of the people have such a natural inclination that they prefer either to remain indifferent or become desperately hostile to any change of religious life in which they have been brought up from their infancy; and also because *the established leaders* of many a religious sect and creed as well as the political rulers, blind with their self interest, try to put every sort of obstacle in the way of the propagator.

It is said that *Akbar* one of the emperors of India once took steps to make a search of truth by examining different religions and consulting with many able men who professed those religions. But, an absolute and despotic monarch though he was, he had not yet sufficient moral courage to declare frankly which of the religions was preferred by him.

Where kings and monarchs tremble to tread, ordinary men can scarcely be expected to take the lead and succeed, unless inspired from within.

Martin Luther says as follows:—

"Had I known when I first began to write, what I now see and find, namely, that people had been such enemies to God's word, and so fiercely had set themselves against the same, truly I had held my peace; for I never should have been so courageous as to have fallen upon the Pope, and to have angered him, and almost the whole christian world with him. I thought at first that people had sinned ignorantly and out of human weakness, and not of set purpose, and willingly to endeavour to suppress God's word; but it pleased God to lead me on in the mouth of the canon like a bar horse that has his eyes blinded and seeth not who runneth upon him. Even so was I, as it were, tugged by my hair to the office of preaching; but had I then known what now I know, ten horses should scarce have driven me to it. Moses and Jeremiah also complained that they were deceived" (Table talk of Martin Luther.)

There are many noble souls in India (especially in the Punjab at the foot of the Himalaya mountain) thoroughly understanding the deep philosophy of religion as well as knowing many hidden laws of nature; but, for considerations like the above, are leading a solitary and passive life of peace and piety. My humble self is also trying to follow them and adopt a similar life; but the thread of my connection with the outer world is not altogether broken, and I am not well-aware of its cause. It may be that I am a beginner yet, or that I have a special bent of mind for "*Reformation,*" or that there is any other mystery of kind Providence in it. It is owing to this thread of connection that I came to know in a *very peculiar way* of the great religious movement started by our American brethren; it is no doubt unparalleled in the history of the world, and gives ample proofs of original thought and power of organization possessed by them.

I have sanguine hopes that if by the grace of God and the exertions of all true religious men, the movement is kept alive for some time, our "Republican brethren" will get full credit for the establishment of a "Republic of conscience," *i e.*, a universal religion acceptable to all conscientious men.

At all events, even in spite of any opposition if raised by self interested men, the seed sown by our divine religionists of the new world, will in process of time grow into the shape of a gigantic tree, spreading its ever-green branches of love and purity, of self denial and philanthropy, throughout all the countries of the world.

It is hoped that at this grand assemblage at Chicago all the sects and creeds shall send in their representatives or in their absence an account of their truths in writing; and if impartially viewed, all religions shall be found replete with Divine truth, though differing from each other, more or less, in external formalities, which is the work of man and therefore liable to constant changes according to the circumstances of the time. If the origin of truths common to all religions is traced, the truths of the Vedas and Shastras will most certainly be found as the parent source.

Although abler men might have gone to Chicago to represent the Vedic truths or sent them in writing, yet I have also taken the liberty to write them, *not for competition's sake, but merely in obedience to the commands of my inner voice;* and I think myself amply repaid for my labours, because I have faithfully served my inner voice; and if one single soul derives any benefit from these pages, it shall, in addition, be a source of real pleasure and satisfaction to me.

It gives me also great pleasure to state that I have been greatly helped and encouraged by many a Divine friend and Holy spirit in the pleasant task of writing these pages. Nevertheless, owing to various causes, I have not been able to dwell upon all the subjects of the Darshanas very exhaustively, only dwelling at length on some of the truths of Yoga Philosophy, which is the favorite subject of my study now-a-days, theoretically as well as practically. What I have written may be considered a collection of un-polished but precious stones out of the inexhaustable mines containing them. But if these truths are well studied and reduced to practice, carefully avoiding all prejudices and preconceptions, and using *Vivek* or discriminative power at every stage of doubt, provocation, or temptation, they can, I believe, greatly help the (जिज्ञासु) or truths seeker to arrive safely at the gate of moksha or that state in which all the functions of the body and the faculties of the mind by harmonious development discharge their proper duties as assigned to them by nature. This state as is evident from the following quotations, and not "अहमब्रह्म" "I am God," or such like beliefs, unfortunately prevalent amongst many of the ignorant classes of India, is considered by our Rishis as affording real happiness or salvation. Patanjali says in part 3rd, Sutra 53 of Yoga Philosophy about salvation thus :—

सत्व पुरुषयोः शुद्धि साम्ये कैवल्य मिति ॥

Sense in English :—

By the purification of Intellect, *i. e.*, by constant right use of Budhi and of all the faculties subordinate to it, and their never going against the naturally pure prusha or soul, leads to salvation.

Again he says in part 4th, Sutra 26.

तदा विवेक निम्नं कैवल्य प्राग्भारं चित्तम् ॥

Sense :—

When chitta or the thinking faculty becomes void of improper desires and wrong notions, it becomes capable of Kaivalya or salvation.

Goutama says (Sutras 21 and 22 Nyaya Philosophy).

बाधना लक्षणं दुःख मिति ॥२॥
तदत्यन्त विमोक्षो पवर्गः ॥२॥

Sense :—(1) Absolute cessation of all pains (they appear only when acting contrary to the nature of any function of the body or faculty of the mind) is salvation.

Vyasji the compiler of Vedant Philosophy defines moksha thus in the 4th part of chapter 4th, sutra 12.

द्वादशाह वदुभयविधिं बादरायणोतः ॥

Sense in English :—

In the state of moksha or salvation there is total absence of pain, ignorance, and all impurities; and the constant presence of real happiness, true knowledge, and all the purities.

The upanishads define moksha or salvation as follows :—

यदा पञ्चावतिष्ठन्ते ज्ञानानि मनसा सह ।
बुद्धिश्च न विचेष्टते तामाहुः परमां गतिम् ॥

Sense :—When the Manas or the will-power with 5 senses realizes the supreme being and acts according to his will, and when the intellect does not work contrary to his own dictates, it is called salvation; it is only "attainable by hard unremitting study amidst the most rigorous asceticism and self mortification and total renunciation of the pleasures of this world."

But to attain the above *salvation* is the most difficult task for man. Of the 3 principal periods of his short life in this transitory world, that of boyhood passes away in utter ignorance, while that of old age is generally full of sickness and misery. The intermediate one or the youth is the time, in which the temptations of the world, most attractive and charming as they seem in out-ward appearance, continually allure him, while the necessities of life keep him engaged in different sorts of work, increasing his wants and woes perpetually. Besides, the *Chitta* or the thinking faculty, with all its subordinate functions, receives an incessant impetus from the residue of past actions in the form of good and bad desires, which if gratified, multiply their number; and if not gratified or partly gratified, keep him extremely uneasy and unhappy. The same has been expressed by a *Western sage* in a very striking manner in the following lines :—

"Man has noble instincts and impulses that impell him to seek the true, to admire the lovely, to worship the good, to feel after and find the Infinite Perfection in which the true, and right, and beautiful, blend into a divine and personal Unity. Man has deep moral convictions of rights that are his due, of duties that he owes, of an enternal law he is bound to discover and obey. Man has sad and remorseful experiences, the sense of unfulfilled duties, of wasted hours, of sorrows that have turned the anticipated joys of his life into utter miseries, of mean and unmanly sins against conscience and heart, against man and God, of losses unredeemed by gain, of the lovely anguish that comes in the hours of bereavement and throws across the life a shadow that no sunshine can pierce. And out of these mingling instincts and impulses, convictions and experiences, rise man's manifold needs, those cravings after rest, those gropings after a strong hand to hold and trust, those cries for pardon, those unutterable groanings after light shed from a Divine face upon his gloom, in which lie at once the greatness and misery of man."

The only way to pass the life successfully in this world and to silence the *Chitta* or the thinking faculty, or in other words to satisfy the soul with all its wants as shown in the above quotation, is to study the Darshanas carefully, and to adopt a life as enjoined therein.

The phrase **धर्मार्थ काम मोक्ष** used in our *prayers* is a hint for gradual improvement and a keynote of harmonious development. It means (Providence grant us) *Dharma* (strength to know the true nature of all the external and internal things and to make a right use of them), *Artha* (wealth) *Kama* (desires), *Moksha* (salvation). First of all Dharma must be acquired, then wealth collected and desires gratified by such means as are not contrary to Dharma. Dharma disappears in proportion the desires either to acquire wealth or to enjoy pleasures predominate; therefore they must always be well-balanced. *Dharma* when associated with Artha and Kama affords *jivan moksha*, but when disassociated with them its fruit is *kaivalya moksha*.

PATANJALI SUTRAS

OR

YOGA PHILOSOPHY.

—:o:—

It is compiled by Patanjali Rishi who was one of the most learned men of his time. He compiled many small books and wrote a commentary upon *Pannini's* grammer, but the principles of *Yoga Philosophy* together with a method of their practice written by Patanjali in the form of *Sutras* or aphorisms made him very conspicuous or rather immortal.

There is a general idea prevalent that yoga can only be practised by quitting the world. This idea prevents many *Grihasthi adhakaris*, or competent persons leading a family life, from making an attempt to practise yoga; while many incompetent persons, incapable of going on well in the world, leave it, pretending that they will practise yoga, little knowing or caring what effects their bad example shall create?

The fact is that by quitting the world is meant to quit the desires, especially the bad desires of the world, gradually and not by a jump.

The sages of antiquity divided life into 4 *ashramas viz:—the Brahmcharya, the Grihastha, the Banprastha* and the *Sanyasa*.

The first Ashrama was a preparation for successful career in the world. It was necessary in it to quit the world, or rather to leave the house of the parents, at the age of 7 or 8 years, for a certain number of years, in order to live with the *guru*, who generally resided in a solitary place, distant from towns and villages. The chief object of this Ashrama was to keep aloof from all the worldly temptations and anxieties, and devote full time, energy, and attention, to the acquirement of knowledge, till the 25th year of age. The illustrious *Sri Krishnaji*, though advanced in age owing to special-circumstances had yet to quit his royal parental roof, for the sake of learning, and to live with his *guru*, like a poor *brahmchari* subsisting on a very frugal food.

The 2nd or the *grihastha ashrama* was to enjoy moderately all the worldly blessings, by an honest way of living, making a right use of all the knowledge acquired in brahmcharya ashrama.

The 3rd or the intermediate ashrama called Banprastha was to be adopted after 50 years of age. It was necessary in it, to turn the attention from all worldly enjoyments, gradually within a period of 25 years, living either in a separate part of his own home, or in the forest where the advantage was to enjoy the *sat-sanga* or the good company of Rishis and Munis ; as well as to teach *Brahmcharis.*

The 4th or the last ashrama was Sanyasa, which was to be adopted by those who successfully passed through the first 3 stages, and had, besides, a real desire for Kaivalya Moksha or *salvation.* They longed to seek the quiet of the forest, living either at the foot of a mountain or on the bank of a river, "renouncing the false ends and empty fictions of common life, and intent upon reunion with the sole reality, the self that is one in all things living."

Since the battle of Mahabharata, which took place in India at a very early (and according to the calculation of the Europeans, pre-historic) period, numerous changes of different sorts, have made the above systems of ashramas very much altered or rather corrupted. The forests of the present day are almost all supervised by Government officials and have scarcely any means of comforts necessary for either the brahmcharya, the bunprastha, or the sanyas ashrama. As a latest example, Guru Nanak, after having been married and blessed with children, felt a desire to practise Yoga, and regenerate India. He quitted grihastha ashrama and practised Yoga, not in the forest, but at Emmnabad, District Gujranwala generally known as "Rori Sahib" and after a long hermitage, he re-adopted "grihastha" in the latter part of his life. Also when teaching certain Yoga Sadhans to a Raja of Ceylon, Guru Nanak prevented the Raja from quitting the world.

Any one having a mind, now, to practise Yoga, must fully consider all the above-mentioned facts, and according to his circumstances, use his discretion in his own special case, *i. e.*, whether to quit the world or otherwise when commencing Yoga practices which are, as far as possible, very clearly detailed below :—

The word *yoga* means '*to join*' and its technical meaning is *communion of the human soul with the supreme soul.* Says the Sutra "योगचित्त वृति निरोध:" that is to say -' by yoga is meant to suppress all the functions of body and mind and thus to be able to join with the supreme being.

Vyasji while commenting upon the above sutra defines *Chitta* or thinking faculty as follows:—

चित नदी नामी भयती वाहिनी वहति कल्याणाय वहति पापाय चयातु कैवल्य प्राग भारा विवेक विषय निम्नासा कल्याण वहा संसार प्राग भारा विवेक विषय निम्ना पाप वहा तत्र वैराग्येण विषय स्रोतः खिली क्रियते विवेक दर्शना भ्यासेन विवेक स्रोत उदघाटयते इत्युभयाधीनश्चित्त वहति निरोध ॥

Sense in English;—

Chitta figuratively speaking is a river flowing with two branches; the one full of *pleasure* and the other full of *pain*; the upper end or the highest stage of the one is *salvation* (and it is very difficult to reach or ascend to it) and it flows down with vivek or discrimination's force into the ocean of innocent enjoyments; the upper end or the highest stage of the other branch is *worldliness* and it flows down with avivek or in-discrimination's force into the ocean of grief. By constant endeavours the former branch must be kept open and the latter shut up; and afterwards attempt should be made to shut up even the latter and try to ascend its source (salvation.)

Patanjali's aphorisms are 190 in number, and are divided into 4 parts. The first part contains 50 aphorisms, the second 58, the third 52, and the fourth 34.

The first part is called *Samadhipad*, because generally speaking it gives a description of samadhis or different kinds of meditation. In this part Patanjali divides yoga into two kinds the *Sampargyata* and *Asampargyata*. To suppress the functions of the chitta by engaging it in the constant study of religious books and discussions with the learned men, and thus improving the faculty of distinguishing right from wrong is the first stage, vitark of the Sampargyata Yoga ; the 2nd is to think over what is learnt in books and in the company of learned men and is called vichar ; the 3rd stage is to realize the value of the knowledge acquired and to feel a sense of joy in meditation and is called anandanugat ; and the 4th is to know and retain his own individuality or self consciousness by means of satvik buddhi or clear understanding and is called asimta anugat. These four stages are called sampargyata, because the chitta has something to meditate upon. But when the above kind of meditation is continued for a long period and with zeal and perseverance, the mind gradually becomes void of all thoughts and Asampargyata Yoga is attained. This Asampargyata Yoga is divided into many kinds such as *Bhava Prattaya Upaya Prattaya*, &c., but the differences between them can only be known to Yogis.

After describing the above kinds of samadhis or meditations, which can only be made use of by the *Uttam adhakaris* or most intellectual or experts, Patanjali suggests some other means for the *maddham adhakaris*, and shall describe *ashtang yoga* for the *beginners* in the 2nd chapter to attain samadhi or meditation. The means are as follows :—

1. By implicit faith in *Iswara* (Providence) who is free from works, afflictions, deserts, and desires, and is altruthful, merciful and just. His symbol is the most sacred but mysterious syllable *OM* (ओ३म्). Those who recite this syllable, thoroughly understanding its meaning and leading a life accordingly, Iswara grants

them in reward a Satvik Buddhi or clear understanding, by means of which they enjoy the choicest blessings of this world and finally succeed in making their soul free from the bondage of body. Briefly speaking, *om* is composed of अ, उ, म, of which अ denotes the *wakeful state* (Jagratavastha) and the whole of the external universe and every thing relating to it; उ denotes the *contemplative state* (Supanavastha) and every thing relative to it; and म denotes the *slumbering state* (Sukhupati avastha) and every thing connected with it. First of all the Yogi should try to reach the *divine spirit* ruling the external nature by making his conduct conform to the laws regulating this universe and identifying his will to that of the Providence, exercising as far as possible the virtues of truthfulness, mercy, justice, cleanliness, self-denial, self-culture, &c. When he keeps himself in this position long enough, the contemplative state will also come in his control and make him in proper time master of the third state too; just as a child if well brought up and educated and made a good child, will also become a good youth and a good old man.

2. By a practice of *Pranayama* or regulation of the breath. This practice if made once a day for five minutes only keeps all the functions of the body and faculties of the mind in full health and proper working order. The breath should be slowly inhaled, suspended for a short time and then exhaled with full force. The process must be repeated as many times as found convenient, but not less than 3 times or more than 101 times in one day.

3. *By concentrating the mind on one particular object in external world.* Any object most attractive and delightful to the mind should be selected and in the beginning the concentration should not last for more than 5 minutes at a time. The practice is generally made three times a day, *i. e.*, in the morning, at noon, and in the evening; the time should never exceed two hours a day.

4. *By concentrating the mind on some internal object of the body,* such as the radient light in the forehead, and observing all the precautions mentioned in the foregoing process.

If the yogi accustoms himself to lead a *passive life* and forgets all the pleasures and pains of this external world as in a dream, or at least does not care much for the temptations and anxieties of the external world, and if all the four sadhans are partly practised at the same time, then the result is most beneficial. Patanjali says that by a regular practice of them, the understanding becomes very clear and attains the grade of *Ritang bhara* (ऋतम्भरा), that is, it always grasps *rit* or truthfulness and becomes far beyond the reach of false notions; after that another stage called *Pragya budhi* (प्रज्ञा बुद्धी) is attained; in which all the seeds of false notions are destroyed, and new seeds of true knowledge grow instead He who possesses this understanding is free from all the cares of this world.

Says the Upanishad :—

प्रज्ञा प्रासाद मारुह्य अशोच्य: शोचतो जनान
भूमिष्ठा निव शैलस्थ: सवान प्राज्ञोनुपश्यति ॥

Sense in English :—

By sitting on the hill of wisdom free from all the troubles of the world, he looks at the miserable people with pity.

The 2nd Part is called *Sadhan Pad.* It gives a full description of the exercises necessary for the performance of yoga and is therefore called the *Kriya yoga* or practical yoga. It commences by saying :—

तप: स्वधयाये श्वर प्रणिधानानि क्रियायोग:

Sense in English :—Kriya yoga consists of :—

1. *Tapa* or asceticism and austerity. Tapa is considered by all our Rishis as the best means for keeping bodily health good, as well as for getting rid of all pains, and of the residua of pains of the previous birth. By Tapa is meant to lead as far as possible a regular life of purity and piety, exercising all the religious rites such as *yamas niyamas, &c.*, with full belief and perseverance, and thus keeping a constant watch and control over all the organs of the body; and not the asceticism and austerity as performed by the

monks and *nuns* of the *old Roman Catholics* or the *severe tortures* inflicted on their body by many an *illiterate* and *ignorant men* of India, nor is it compulsory for the practitioner of Tapa or any other religious exercises or yoga sadhans to lead a *single life*, on the contrary, a wife has often been found a most useful companion by all those Rishis, who, led a *married life*, performing their Tapas and other religious exercises in company with their *Ardhangi* or *better half*. *Badrayna Rishi*, the son of *Badri Rishi*, the compiler of *Vedanta Darshana* and his wife were undergoing the severest kinds of *Tapas* when their illustrious son, *Shukha Deva* was born. *Gautama Rishi*, the compiler of *Nyaya philosophy* was the husband of noble *Ahalya*, and even the great yogi *Patanjali* himself was a married man, his wife's name being Lolupa.

In ancient times the designation *Sadhu* was generally given to those who used to perform the above kinds of Tapas. *Maharaja Ram Chandra* was frequently addressed by his spiritual guide, *Vasishtaji*, as *Sadhu* ; while unfortunately at present, it is applied to those who quit their home and relations, generally under some difficulty or temptation, and instead of performing true Tapas lead an idle life of ignorant bliss or sin.

Figuratively speaking human body is described as a *chariot*, the *senses* as *horses*, *manas* as driver, the *atma or soul* as a king sitting in the chariot with *buddhi or intellect* as his attendant. The *world* is compared to a road runing from Heaven to Hell ; Heaven being situated on the higher ground in the north, and hell on the lower ground in the south ; so it is difficult to ascend to Heaven, but "easy is the descent to Hell." To drive the *chariot* northward with proper speed, *i. e.*, neither too swiftly nor too slowly although making the speed sometimes more and sometimes less at discretion, and constantly examining and making necessary repairs in the chariot, as well as keeping a full control over the horses, &c. ; and bravely facing all the difficulties coming into the way, is in reality the proper exercise of Tapa.*

* The Katha Upanishad compares the body with a car, the soul with a rider, the senses with horses, the mind with the rein, &c.

(2). *Swadhiyaya* or constant study of religious books; it is one of the most important and also compulsory exercise for achieving success in yoga practice. Vyasji defines swadhiyaya as :—

"मोक्ष शास्त्राणाम अध्ययनम प्रणव जपो वा"

Sense —To read those books which make mention of salvation and to recite the syllable *om* which is the indicator of the divinity Iswara; the upanishads put *great* importance to this exercise in the following verse :—

स्वाध्यायात योगमासीत योगात स्वाध्यायमामनेत।
स्वाध्याय योग सम्पत्या परमात्मा प्रकाश्यते ॥

Sense—To accomplish meditation by the help of Swadhiyaya and to make the exercise of Swadhiyaya by the help of meditation and by the strength and union of both of them divine wisdom is attained and Supreme Being known.

(3). *Iswara parnidhan* or full devotion to God.

Vyasji says :—

देवा ऋषयः सिद्धाश्च स्वाध्याय शीलस्य
दर्शनं गच्छन्ति कार्यि चासय वर्त्तते ॥

Sense.—Divine souls interview the exerciser of स्वाध्याय and help him.

This kriya yoga if observed rigidly, all subsequent exercises can be performed very easily; and by its regular practice all the afflictions gradually disappear. Afflictions are numerous and have been classified by Patanjali into five parts *viz* :—

अविद्या अस्मिता राग द्वेषाभिनिवेशाः पञ्च क्लेशाः

Sense—Ignorance, egotism, desire, aversion, and a fear from death and a love for living for ever; of these अविद्या or ignorance is the most dreadful and is called by our Rishis as the parent of all afflictions. Patanjali thinks ignorance to consist chiefly in looking upon the false pleasures of this world as sources of true happiness. The above mentioned afflictions arise from attachment to worldly affairs and create a desire to do Karma or actions which lead behind them, their seeds or residua to be worked out in the next birth and in that next birth other actions are done and their residua left behind, and thus the wheel of transmigration keeps itself revolving perpetually, unless the chitta is stopped and prevented from doing its work by the necessary yoga practices.

Many of our educated brethren of the present day hesitate to believe in the theory of the transmigration of souls; but if they will impartially and dispassionately think over the arguments of our Rishis, they will most probably be inclined to accept the probability of the theory. One of the arguments is that as "neither virtue nor vice always brings on its deserts in this life, so the necessity for a next life becomes unavoidable; and if the soul was to have a next corporeality of some kind to bear the deserts, there was nothing to hinder the transmigration many times."

Gautama Rishi the compiler of the Nyaya Philosophy says:—

"पुनरुत्पत्तिः प्रत्यभावः"

Sense in English:—

One coming into existence is sure to die, and equally sure to come into èxistence again; to disappear from one body and re-appear in another is called Pratiyabhava.

Some raise the *question* that if transmigration be believed as true, then why do people not remember the events of their previous birth? The reply is that when the pains and pleasures and other accidents of childhood are not remembered, how then, one can reasonably expect with his limited memory overburdened with ten thousand passions and anxieties, to remember the deeds of his previous birth. If, however, one be really desirous to know this hidden law of nature, he must throw off the burden of passions and anxieties and leading a regular pure and pious life must practise yoga.

Another *objection* generally raised is that Iswara or Providence cannot be called just and merciful when He punishes and rewards souls, without letting them know the deeds for which they are so punished or rewarded. The answer is that though people in the plains below do not know when it rains on the hills, yet when they notice rivers over-flowing they make an inference that rain has fallen on the hills; similarly if the chief or ultimate cause of the unequal distribution of happiness and misery be traced, it will be found no other than the deeds of previous birth. Suppose a physician and an ignorant villager are laid up with fever; the former at once traces the cause or causes of his sickness; but the latter in many cases does not know the particular cause of his illness, generally knowing only this much that the illness is due to some intemperance or other; but both will equally feel the pains of fever which is of course the effect of some intemperate cause. If then, the villager were to complain that Iswara is unjust, because He made him sick without letting him know the cause of sickness, his complaint would not be considered reasonable.

It must be borne in mind that it is very difficult to trace the *cause* of an *effect*; for generally one effect has not only one cause, but several causes as its back ground; while those several causes are in themselves the effects of other previous causes and so on. Again the relation of cause and effect becomes further complicated because all the pain and pleasure that are experienced in life are effects not only of the events of previous birth, but also of the deeds of present life.

A 3rd *objection* though very futile in itself, is raised that it is very degrading and horrible to think that owing to transmigration a man would become a rat or *vice versa*. The reply is that in nature changes take place gradually; a human being has more likelihood of receiving a similar body in his next birth, and if he leads a life of piety and virtue he is sure to receive a better body and better chances for enjoying the blessings of life.

All the Schools of Indian Philosophy have believed fully in the theory of transmigration and have tried to devise means for breaking this chain, and proclaimed in different forms and shapes that the chain can only be broken by *cancelling bad thoughts* and *deeds* by good ones; by *leading a pious* and *virtuous life*; and *finally* by *becoming absorbed* in *meditation* and finding out the *most holy* and *all-pervading Brahm*, within his own *pure soul*.

Patanjali proves by a striking illustration that the cause of transmigration are the above-mentioned five afflictions. For instance, *ignorance* leads to commit a sin, punishment for that sin comes either in the present or in the next birth, and while the punishment is being borne, another sin is committed and so on. The same arguments can be applied to the other 4 *afflictions*. It must also be remembered that it is not only the affliction or the bad deed which necessitates transmigration, but the good deeds do equally cause birth and re-birth. In this respect, our Rishis call bad deeds as *fetters* made of *iron* and good deeds as *fetters* made of *gold*. For supposing instead of committing a sin, a good act is done, it is very necessary to enjoy the fruit of that good act in the next birth if not in the present, and in that next existence other good acts are performed which necessitate a third existence and so on. In fact every action good or bad bears its fruits and causes another birth and the succession recurs without limit.

This is another truth which is generally ridiculed and looked upon with contempt by many men of Western thoughts. To an ordinary man, of course, the idea of giving up good works and calling them as fetters would seem absurd unless he understands the spirit of the truth.

First of all he must know that by good action is meant *sakam karmas* and there is a higher class of action than these good actions *viz., niskam karmas*, or good actions done for goodness sake. This latter class of action is required to be done for the whole of the life time.

As for good actions done with a view to enjoy their fruits, *viz.*, the pleasures of the world, experience shows that they are intermingled with pains like roses and thorns and therefore it is safer and wiser for one who is really ambitious to rise in the world and wishes to get rid of afflictions, to consider both the *good* and *bad action* as *fetters*; and giving them up must devote his full attention to *niskam karmas*. All the great men of India, nay of the whole world, have only been able to perform works of permanent character and to discover noble truths in different departments of knowledge, when they have turned a deaf ear to sakama karmas and their fruits, the false and fleeing pleasures of the world. Besides, the fruits of Sakama karmas or good actions are pleasures of the world, which when repeatedly enjoyed lose their zest and look like pains, and decidedly they are pains in comparison with meditation and other *niskam* karmas the fruit of which is eternal bliss.

There is an old *Ithihas* or tradition that *Jaigishava Rishi* who by the practice of Yoga got knowledge of his *previous births* was once asked by one *Adya Rishi* as to what *pleasures* he enjoyed in previous births. Jaigishava replied that he never enjoyed any pleasures; Adya Rishi again questioned that without possessing good qualities like truthfulness, honesty, justice, benevolence, &c., and without performing good actions and enjoying their inevitable fruits, the pleasures of the world, Jaigishava could not have been able to practise yoga and get knowledge of his previous births; Jaigishava replied that certainly he enjoyed the fruits of his good actions which were at the time of enjoyment felt as pleasures; but they seem to him now in comparison with his blissful state (kaivalya) as pains.

Similarly the illustrious *Buddha* son of a king and the founder of a great living religion, *Buddhism*, after many hardships and full experience in every sphere of life, discovered this noble truth and taught it to his disciples that all the pleasures of the world (which are of course the fruits of sakam karmas or good actions) are anitya, dukh, anath or transient, sorrowful, and un-real, and that "existence is suffering" and transmigration a curse and the ultimate object of every noble soul must be to get rid of it. Says Buddha:—

"Birth is attended with pain, old age is painful, disease is painful, death is painful, association with the un-pleasant is painful, separation from the pleasant is painful, the non-satisfaction of one's desire is painful, in short the coming into existence is painful." The origin of the pain is traced to the desire to live for ever, or the *abhinavesha* affliction of the Patanjali's Yoga Philosophy, as well as a desire to gratify passions. The method suggested by the holy Buddah for suppressing the pains or the origin of suffering is the destruction of passions and desires and then to try to reach Nirvana or the kaivalya moksha of the Yoga Philosophy. An eminent Western Philosopher who studied our philosophy attentively and found it original and a source of solace to him, after dwelling upon the miseries of existence and showing that even suicide* (which is so common in the so called civilized countries) was not enough to put a stop to the miseries, suggests that salvation can only be had by "knowing that the world is radically and essentially bad. Such knowledge leaves no ground for that old affirmation of the will to live, it leads to a negation of will, to a renunciation of desire, which completed by means of asceticism and mortification, must attain that perfect freedom of will, that true Nirvana or Kaivalya, in which there is no more will, therefore, no longer an ideal presentation of a real world."

Good actions, however, should not be considered as fetters and *given up* unless the niskam karmas are *well caught hold of.*

Patanjali suggests the following means to avoid bad as well as good actions. He says that an act once performed must bear its fruit good or bad; it is a rule of the Impartial and Just Providence and cannot be broken even by Himself, much less so by a mortal being, be he a prophet or a seer. But it is in the power of every man to avoid doing such actions as bear fruits, *i. e.*, the nisheda and sakam karmas or bad and good actions, (their detail is given in 4th part.) But they cannot be avoided, unless the relation which the *Intellect* bears to *Soul* and the true position of both are known. The relation is as follows:—

* Our Shastras consider *suicide* as one of the greatest *sins*.

The *Intellect* is like a spectacle and has the form of elements and organs and is for the purpose of experience. In it lies liberation of the soul or its confinement. *Soul* is the spectator and though in its nature it is pure, perfectly pure, yet when conjoined with the intellect and its subordinate organs, soul beholds the intellectual ideas and feels pleasure and pain. Soul thinks it is the experiencer and intellect thinks itself to be the experience. By profound meditation, in asampragyata yoga the above false notion disappears, and intellect merges into the soul and ceases to think itself the experiencer. The knowledge by which this conclusion is arrived at is divided into 7 grades by Patanjali. In the 1st grade the yogi thinks that the knowledge has been acquired by him; in the 2nd he feels that nothing more remains to be known; in the 3rd he thinks that he has overcome all his afflictions; in the 4th he thinks that he is thoroughly in possession of vivek or discriminative knowledge. In this grade he is able to solve any complicated religious problem by the help of the vivek. These four grades when duly achieved liberate the yogi from sakam karmas, not the least desire for doing any work which bears fruit is left in him. It is called kriya vimukti. The 5th grade makes him convinced that his intellect has accomplished its purpose; in the 6th grade the well known and most powerful 3 qualities called satwa, sajas, and tamas or tranquility, activity, and darkness* cease to operate upon him; and in the 7th grade the intellect goes back into the soul and the latter is perfectly liberated and the chitta vimukti or the liberation of the soul from the bondage of intellect and its subordinate organs takes place.

After giving a brief description of the *Intellect* and *Soul* and the mode of *liberation*, Patanjali, for the sake of beginners, suggests more practical and easy means by which all the *impurities* of the body and mind and particularly those of the former (मल), and all the *agitations* of the chitta विक्षेप would be removed and the *understanding* would become clear in the highest degree. The means alluded to are 8 in number *viz* :—

---

* Their detail is given in the Sankhya Philosophy.

(*1*) *Yama*, (*2*) *Niyama*, (*3*) *Asan*, (*4*) *Pranayama*, (*5*) *Prattihara*, (*6*) *Dharna*, (*7*) *Dhyan*, and (*8*) *Samadhi* ; of these the first five are called *Bahiranga* or external exercises and are explained in this part, while the last three are called Antaranga or internal exercises and are explained in the 3rd part.

Although it is advisable that all the yoga sadhans must be practised under the immediate supervision and guidance of an efficïent teacher, yet it is *imperatively* necessary to practise this *ashtang yoga* with the help of a yogi.

The word *yama* literally means to restrain and technically it stands for the following five exercises.

“ तत्रा हिंसा सत्यास्तेयब्रह्म चर्या परिग्रहायमा ”

Explanation :—

The 1st exercise is *Ahinsa*, *i. e.*, not to injure any living being with thought, utterance or action. Ahinsa is divided into 21 parts, and great discretion is required to exercise them. For instance, it is not against Ahinsa to injure or even kill any living being for self-defence, or for the defence of a number of other living beings, or for the safety of a nation or country, but endeavours must be made to avoid such opportunities. By a proper application of Ahinsa all living creatures become as friends ; even the angry lion and poisonous snake lose their natural propensities, and become like a harmless goat and inoffensive worm when they come in cc act with the person who is much advanced in his exercise of Ahinsa. The 2nd sadhan is *Satya* or truthfulness. Every body likes to speak the truth, but it is very difficult to know what is truth ; besides, there are so many temptations and so many series of previous untruthful deeds that one scarcely dares speaking the truth. Our shastras have prescribed certain test by which truth can easily be ascertained. Generally speaking truth is that which does not undergo any change, *i. e.*, remains unaltered in past, present, and future times, and is not contrary to the laws of nature or the instinct of human being, provided that instinct is void of partiality and self-interest. The method suggested to speak the truth is to consult the *innerself* or conscience before doing an action or uttering a word. The more is the innerself consulted and obeyed, the more will the habit of speaking the truth be achieved, and strength gained to resist the temptations; also the series of previous untruthful deeds gradually lessens, and the person becomes thoroughly truthful. The 3rd exercise called *Astyai* means not to steal or intend stealing another's property. The motto "It is a sin to steal a pin" must always be remembered. If any thing is awfully needed or allure the mind excessively endeavours should be made to gain it by *fair* and *proper means* and not by *theft or usurpation.* The well known *six causes** by which the world has come into existence, if well understood and well applied, can supply without fail all the necessities of life.

A continued practice of this sadhan (astyai) reduces the wants to a very limited number of things, and the mind obtains some special powers by which those few wants, which are of course of the highest nature, and which gradually decrease in number, are invariably supplied by the kind Providence.

And at last the desires of the lower order giving place to those of the highest ones, no desire remains, and it is at this stage that flashes of Divine Wisdom now and then begin to penetrate into his mind, by which he understands that all the luxuries of the world are full of misery; and that the necessities of life such as air, water, &c., &c., are supplied by Providence to all the living beings in equal proportion; that the wearing of too many clothes and the living in large buildings and palaces, deprive the organs of breathing and touch, *i. e.*, lungs and skin from receiving open and pure air, and that the eating of too many things, *i. e.*, a luxurious and irritant diet brings innumerable diseases, &c., &c. By attaining the above knowledge with full conviction he prefers living by nature to living by the so called civilized arts and luxuries; and in course of time comes to know further that there are very few real wants and com-

---

* कर्म चेष्टा, समय, विद्या, पुरुषार्थ, सामग्री, संकल्प

forts supplied by the external world, and that the source of every comfort and pleasure lies within his own self.

The 4th sadhan is Brahmcharya which means to suppress the lust and observe chastity. Brahmcharya consists of 8 parts, *viz.*—to avoid bad company, bad talk, bad thought, the reading of immoral books, the singing or hearing of immoral songs, visiting the opposite sex in solitary place or at undue time, co-habiting, and destroying the semen in any other way. This Sadhan if welll observed from the childhood confers all the blessings of the world ; but if not cared for at that age, it is very difficult or almost impossible to mend the mature wild habits. Brahmcharya affords greatest pleasure and violating it inflicts greatest sufferings.

The 5th sadhan is *Aprigraha, i. e.*, not to indulge in vanity. After performing the above-mentioned sadhans for a long time and possessing all the virtues and powers resulting from them, if one does not become proud and continues devoting the whole of his time in their performance one comes to know the *events of his previous births.*

These exercises must be followed one by one, and along with them the following 5 sadhans of *Niyama* must also be observed.

"शौच सन्तोष तपः स्वाध्यायेश्वर प्रणिधानानि नियमाः"

The 1st is *shoucha* or cleanliness. Food, house, cloth, and outer body or skin must be cleaned by water ; daily bathing is very neces[illegible]y. Teeth must be cleaned before bathing by Danta Dhavan or a small fresh twig of some tree such as kikar, nim, &c., stomach must be kept clean by regularly answering the calls of nature, as well as by keeping a fast either once a week, once a fortnight, or at the most once a month ; blood must be kept clean and in proper circulation by Vyayama or proper bodily exercise in which all the body would perspire.

The 2nd sadhan is *santosha* or contentment. It must always be borne in mind that the just and merciful Providence has appointed every man's station in life according to his previous deeds and thoughts, and constantly keeps it changed according to the exertions of the present life. So instead of bewailing the misfortune every body must try to remove them by proper exertions; a contended mind is said to be a hidden treasure and a guard from trouble. The yogi should try to reduce his wants to the bare necessities and should accustom himself to be satisfied and contended under all circumstances.

The 3rd sadhan is Tapa or asceticism, the 4th Swaddhiyaya or reading of religious books, and the 5th Iswara pernidhana or faith in Providence. These last 3 sadhans have already been explained in aphorism I of this part, where they are counted as independent exercises for a maddham adhakari or middle class practitioner.

The 3rd exercise of the ashtang yoga is *asan*, which means posture while in meditation. Patanjali says:—

"तत्र स्थिर सुखमासनम्" सूत्र ४६ ॥

Which means the posture in which mind is at greatest ease. But any kind of posture, however difficult it may be, appears to be easy when one is accustomed to it. Patanjali has not specified any kind of posture, but many of the commentators as well as practitioners of the modern times have described about 84 different sorts of postures, of which some 4 are most in common use by advanced yogis, and their diagram has been given by me in Gayan Dipka, an urdu pamphlet compiled by me.

The 4th exercise is *Pranayama* or the regulation of the breath. The process to begin with has already been explained. Patanjali has prescribed four grades of Pranayama and it is in the fourth grade that the whole of the body with senses and understanding attains perfect health. Patanjali says:—

प्राणायामाद अशुद्धिक्षये ज्ञान दीप्तिरा विवेक ख्याते ॥

Sense in English:—

By a practice of pranayama all the impurities of body, senses, and intellect gradually vanish, and true knowledge penetrates into the mind, until salvation is attained.

The 5th sadhan is called *Prattihara* or the abstraction of the organs. Technically it means that all the organs especially those of hearing and sight should be turned from their external usual food, *i. e.*, the sound and sight in the external world, to the internal unusual food. I have already explained this process in the body of my letter. By this process the organs of senses merge into their primary cause, the manas or the organ of will-power. It is at this stage that the preliminary or external exercises of yoga end. After this yoga proper commences, in which a direct battle, without the intervention of senses, is fought with the *manas*, *chitta* and *buddhi* by means of *dharna*, *dhyan* and *samadhi*. The detail of this yoga proper is given in the 3rd and 4th parts.

The 3rd Part in called *vibhuti pad* because it treats of certain results of the yoga practices of the secondary nature called *siddhis* or extraordinary powers and faculties. It opens by defining the 6th exercise *dharna* or steadfastness thus :—

"देशबन्धश्चित्तस्य धारणा" Sutra 1.

Sense in English :—

To confine chitta or the thinking faculty to one particular object; no particular object is described by Patanjali; but generally the attention is fixed in *trikuti* or where 3 lights meet in a triangular form in the forehead. This fixation when steadfastly done is called *dhyan* or contemplation. When *dhyan* is more intense and loses its identity it is called *samadhi* or profound meditation.

In fact these three practices are one and the same, the difference is only of degrees. When they are practised successively, they are called *sanyama*. A constant practice of sanyama produces many extraordinary powers in the manas, chitta, and buddhi. These powers as a first result of meditation are granted by Providence to enable the yogi to reach the highest stage, *salvation*. If therefore they are not properly used to clear the way for salvation, and are abused by making a display of them to the wordly men, the *siddhis acquired by so hard a labour*, shall all disappear bye and bye. There are many temptations and obstacles that come in the way of the yogi. One of the most degrading temptations prevalent now a days is that many ignorant and selfish men try to derive undue benefit from the siddhis of the yogi. If the yogi makes a display of his siddhis they disappear; if he denies to do so those worldly men are disappointed and put obstacles in his way. It is a custom with the ignorant public and even with the worldly wise men that when hopeful of getting some benefit from the yogi, they puff him with praise and offer him wealth, &c., but when disappointed, back-bite him and try to create his enemies and put him to numerous troubles. There are also other temptations of a higher nature that come in the way of the yogi. He must therefore leave no stone unturned to escape from all the temptations and thus save himself from many unnecessary troubles. The best advice for him is to keep his siddhis as secret as possible. I do not think it advisable to give any detail of the siddhis; for any person practising the exercises mentioned in the preceding part will come to know them himself.

The 4th Part is called *kaivalya pad,* because it treats of the subject of moksha or salvation, by which the soul is made free from all bondage.

This part is the most important and contains many deep philosophical theories which are discussed in the form of questions and answers.

The 1st question raised is whether samadhi has any influence over the *external body* and can make it *changed.* The answer given is that all the elements of the material body undergo changes according to the laws of nature incessantly, and meditation adds *facility* to *remove all obstacles from their way*; just as a cultivator of ground levels the surface of the soil of his fields, and removes all inequalities out of the channel of water, and then the water according to the laws of gravitation comes itself flowing down into the field. Another question is raised asking whether the powers attained by meditation, *i. e.*, siddhis, are similar to those attained through other causes, *e. g.*, birth or exertion, or are they different from them. The reply given in aphorism 6 is that they are different. The powers attained through other causes have their connection chiefly with the former existence, the residua of previous births give them life; but the siddhis or powers achieved by meditation have no support from previous birth, and likewise they do not produce any after-consequences which other causes do.

Here Patanjali divides karmas or actions into 4 *classes, viz*:. *white or virtuous, black or vicious*, a *mixture* of both virtuous and vicious, and *neither virtuous nor vicious, i. e., niskam*; of these the 1st 3 kinds of actions leave their residua behind them, but the 4th class of actions do not leave any residua behind them, and yogis always perform the *last class* of actions.

The fruit or the after-consequences of the above-mentioned 3 classes of actions are two fold; *instinct* and *kind, age* and *experience.* The philosophy of *instinct* is the most beautiful and logical. It is described thus:—

"Every action, every sensation, and every form of experience leaves on chitta or the thinking faculty an impress of its own, and such impressions accumulating in course of a life time become the stock of residua, which though for the time being latent, are susceptible of revival by proper stimulants in subsequent existences. This revival is instinct, *i. e.*, instead of believing instinct to be spontanious, self evolved, &c., &c., our Rishis take it to be the fruit of the remembrance of former existence revived by particular circumstances."; the other 3 technical words *kind, age*, and *experience* are explained thus:—

Accordihg to the residua of the former life one is doomed to be born either in a higher or a lower grade; this is called *kind.* The long or short period of life which is fixed according to one's deserts is called *age.* Pain and pleasure felt in that period of life are called *experience.*

A question is then raised as to how the first birth took place. The reply given is that soul and matter are eternal and therefore have no beginning or first birth. This theory of eternity is also one of the most logical theories.

If it were admitted that *God* created the universe, then the necessity would arise of making *Him* engaged in karma or action and bear its fruit. But God is perfectly free from afflictions, actions, deserts, and desires; and therefore the universe cannot be called as created by Him. If the universe were stated to be *self-involved* then the theory of "*nothing comes from nothing*" would not allow it.

A question is again raised that if eternity is established and the desires are said not to have an eternal course, how then can they be removed, and if they are not removed, transmigration would not end? The reply given is that अविद्या or not knowing the true nature of things is the *primary cause* of *desires*; the effect is *body* and its *tendencies* towards perishable enjoyment; and *chitta* or the thinking faculty gives support to the body; therefore if chitta is stopped from action, the desires shall also cease and no new residua shall be produced and thus freedom shall be attained.

Another objection is raised to the following effect that chitta is liable to changes; it cannot be in one existence what it was before and therefore it is not eternal. The objection is removed by saying that every thing in this world is eternal, nothing is either created or destroyed. *Birth* and *death* are only changes of attributes and therefore when chitta undergoes a change in one state, it reverts either to its former state or adopts a new one. The change in the chitta takes place owing to the influence of the 3 qualities *Sattwa*, *Rajas* and *Tamas* These qualities have a succession of predominence between themselves; and when one of them has more influence the remaining two merge into it. Therefore if a person carefully tries to create more influence in the quality of Sattwa or tranquility, so long as that quality is predominent he will remain *happy* and chitta shall remain functionless to a great extent. Another question is raised, that as there is no stability in chitta, so knowledge derived by perception cannot be constant. The reply is that the *real perceiver* is soul, which is *unchangeable* and therefore the knowledge gained by the soul through chitta is constant.

Soul being constantly present in the body witnesses all the actions of nature, which take place in all the innermost functions and structures nay in every *pramanu* or atom in the body.

When by a proper and continued exercise of yoga, the philosophy of *soul and intellect, chitta and manas* is well understood, all the false thoughts and deeds disappear, the 3 qualities cease to operate, and the soul realizing the all pervading and all supporting Brahm within itself, abides in its own essence. This is salvation and to attain it is the ultimate object of the Yoga Philosophy.

THE SANKHYA PHILOSOPHY.

This system of philosophy is much akin to that of *yoga.* It is compiled by *Kapila Rishi* who is believed to be a *born philosopher.* Many religious men of high reputation are of opinion that there were different theories of religious philosophy current in Kapila's time, and the master mind of Kapila put them all in a systematical form, and named it *Sankhya Darshana.* Kapila has described *Prakriti* or matter in its subtle form as made up of 3 qualities, tranquility, activity and darkness, respectively. Then 23 tattavas or entities are counted up as spontaneously coming out of prakriti just as cream comes out of milk, or milk out of cow; prusha or soul is described as the 25th, but quite distinct from prakriti, though through the influence of the above mentioned 3 qualities of prakriti, prusha feels pleasure and pain when confined in the body.

Kapila's philosophy is written in the form of sutras or aphorisms and is divided into six chapters. The 1st chapter contains 164 sutras; the 2nd 47; the 3rd 84; the 4th 32; the 5th 129; and the 6th 70 sutras.

Briefly speaking the *first chapter* explains what the terms *bandha* and *moksha* or confinement and salvation mean. The *2nd chapter* solves the riddle of the universe, *i. e.*, how it exists, beginning with the eternal germ prakriti, or matter. Also prusha or soul is described as eternal and unchangeable and that all changes take place in prakriti, though Prusha seems to be influenced by them. The soul regulates all the functions of the body equally, but *buddhi or intellect,* the highest product of prakriti, is in soul's immediate command and in direct contact. This is well explained in the following 47th sutra:—

समान कर्म योगे बुद्धे प्राधान्यं लोक वल्लोकवत् ॥

Sense :—Although soul has an equal influence over all the senses, &c., yet its foremost connection is with the intellect just as a Raja has an equal connection with his subjects but it is only his mantri (secretary) who comes in his contact most frequently.

The *3rd chapter* gives a full description of the 5 grosser elements called mahabhuta and also explains the two kinds of the body, *i. e.*, sthula and sukshama or coarse and subtle. The elements are as follows :—(1) *Akasha* or ether, its quality is *sound* and organ of sense, *ear*. (2) *vayu* or air, quality *trangibility*, organ of sense, *skin*. (3) *Taijas* or heat and light, quality *colour*, organ of sense, *eye*. (4) *Apas* or water, quality *taste*, organ of sense, *tongue*. (5) *Prithivi* or earth, quality *smell*, organ of sense, *nose*. The *sthula* or outer body consists of (1) *ras* or chyle, (2) *rakht* or blood, (3) *mans* or flesh, (4) *meda* or fat, (5) *asthi* or bone, (6) *majja* or marrow, and (7) *shukr* or semen. The *sukshama* or inner body consists of (1) 5 *prans* or vital powers, (2) 5 *karma indrayas* or organs of action, (3) 5 *gyan indrayas* or organs of sense, and (4) *anthakran chatushtaya* or *manas*, *buddhi*, *chitta*, and *ahankara* (organ of will-power, intellect, thinking faculty, and self consciousness).

The *4th chapter* contains some moral lessons full of allusions and illustrations. These moral lessons seem to me so useful that I think it will not be out of place if I quote a few of them here.

राज पुत्रवत् तत्वोपदेशात् (1)

Sense :—By right knowledge one becomes like the son of the Raja. The allusion is that a certain Raja's son was stolen away in infancy by a Bheel or thief tribe man. The child having been brought up in Bheels' family believed himself to be one of them, but when he came to know that he was a Raja's son, all of a sudden his inclinations of theft like habits vanished. In like manner man on getting right knowledge shall know his real nature.

आवृत्तिर सकृ दुपदेशात् (3)

Sense :—If discriminative knowledge (vivek) is not obtained by one (updesh) advice, such advice should be repeated just as *Shuvet ketu* received repeated instructions from *Aruni* and other *Munis*.

पिता पुत्र वदुभ्योर्दृष्टत्वात् (4)

Vivek points out to both the Prusha and Prakriti just as the mother of a child, who was born and brought up when his father was away from home, pointed out to the child his father and to the father his child.

छिन्नहस्तवद्वा (7)

When bad desires are extinguished by vivek, they never recur, just as when a hand is cut off from the body, no desire is felt to put it back there.

बहुशास्त्र गुरूपासनेपि सारादानं षटपदवत् (13)

Out of the many shastras and the many instructions received from the Guru (religious teacher) those only should be remembered and adopted which create vivek, just as a honey-bee visits many flowers and picks the honey.

कृतनियमलङ्घ नादानर्थक्यं लोकात् (15)

Cleanliness and other practices necessary for obtaining vivek, if not well observed do not produce any result just as a patient, if not obeying the physician's directions seldom derives any benefit from medicine.

प्रणति ब्रह्मचर्योपसर्पणानि कृत्वासिद्धिर्बहु कालात् तद्वत (19)

By humility and observing perfect chastity and going to his teacher to read the Vedas, and by a continuance of these practices for a long time, vivek is obtained just as *Indra* obtained it.

This is an Allegorical allusion, full mention of which is made in the Chhandogya upanishad chapter 8, seccion 7th to 12th. Once upon a time *Indra* or Maghawan among the Devas or enlightened faculties, and *Virochana* among the Asuras or faculties covered with tama or darkness, went to *Prajapati* to learn the philosophy of *soul.* When they lived with him for 32 days (and not

32 years as is believed by some), Prajapati asked them, "With what intent do you abide here." They replied. "To know *soul*, which is said to be free from the *sin, decay, death or repinning.*" "It is the being you perceive within the eye; it is Brahm, the deathless and fearless" said Prajapati. By this a certain yoga sadhan is alluded to.

Virochana took it literally and instructed the Asuras to *adore* the *outer body*. It is in the nature of man to grasp the easier part of the truth first; and this is one of the chief reasons why ordinary men follow the formalities of religion more readily and zealously, than the deep mysteries of it.

Indra, however, practised the sadhan and saw the *inner shadow*, but as it looked sometimes clear and sometimes unclear and at other times disappeared altogether, Indra doubted of its being *deathless*, and informed Prajapati of his doubts, who was glad to hear them and promised to explain soul again, directing Indra to stay for 32 days more and practise yoga. After which Prajapati explained soul as that which enjoys the dreamy state. It is an allusion to the *Dyhanavastha* of the yoga. Indra rigidly following these instructions came to know that fear, grief, &c., are felt by the enjoyer of the dream, but soul is called fearless. With this doubt he again approached Prajapati, who after 32 days stay, again explained soul as that in which retiring, the sleeper does not dream and is at full rest. By this *samadhi* of the yoga is alluded to. Indra after realizing samadhi state, again came to Prajapati and said that the soul pointed out seemed to be quite un-conscious of its own self, as if dead for the time, and therefore can hardly be called *deathless*.

Prajapati again promised to explain soul and asked Indra to stay for 5 days more. This time the period is shortened from 32 to 5 days, because after samadhi, asampragyata yoga, in which the soul is realized as fully conscious, is attained only with a little exertion. After 5 days Prajapati explained soul as quite distinct from the body, the latter being only an instrument for its enjoyment. Soul is *manifest* when it comesocct innta with the material objects, and un-manifest when it retires to the innermost recesses of the body. Intellect is the celestial eye of the soul, which when once beholds the soul in the innermost recesses of the body, by the practice of asampragyata yoga, can always after that behold it in outer world as well

Any able disciple if living with an able teacher for 101 days as Indra did, can learn yoga and understand the philosophy of *soul.*

न काल नियमो वाम देववत् (20)

No limit of time can be fixed for obtaining vivek. *Vam Deva Rishi* owing to his good sanskars (residua of former actions) got vivek in a very short space of time.

विरक्तस्य हेय हानमुपादेयो पादनं हंस क्षीरवत् (23)

He who has got vivek, must always use it by giving up certain things (worldly pleasures) and adopting others (the path of salvation) just as a swan separates water from the milk and drinks the latter.

नभोगाद्राग शान्तिर्मुनिवत् (27)

The more the pleasures are enjoyed the more thirst is felt for them just as was the case with *Saubhari* सौभरि *muni* who remarked at the time of his death that.

"आमृत्युतो नैव मनोरथानामन्तो सित विज्ञातमिदं मयाद्य ।
मनोरथा सक्ति परस्य चित्तं न जायते वै परमार्थ सङ्गी" ॥

I have known it well to-day that desires never end tIll death ; and the mind which is full of passions and desires can never receive the reflections of *true knowledge.*

The 5th Chapter repeats many a truth and theory already explained in the foregoing chapters in the form of questions and answers. The 6th or the last chapter explains in an exhaustive way what the siddhanta or established conclusion and belief of the compiler is ; and ends with the following sutra.

यद्वा तद्वा तदुच्छित्तिः पुरुषार्थ स्तदुच्छित्तिः पुरुषार्थः (70)

Sense :—Whatever may be the connection between Prusha and Prakriti, it must at all cost be broken, in order to get rid of the 3 fold pains.

This last sutra of the last chapter has a connection with the first sutra of the first chapter, which is as follows :—

अथ त्रिविधदुःखात्यन्तनिवृत्तिरत्यन्त पुरुषार्थः (1)

Sense :—A complete deliverance from three fold pains is the summum bonum. All the pains existing in this world are classified into 3 kinds, *viz* :—

(1) आध्यात्मिक or pains arising from bodily sickness or mental agitation.

(2) आधिभौतिक or pains sustained through other living beings such as jealous and envious men, ferocious animals, poisonous reptiles, &c., &c.

(3) आधिदैविक or pains felt under the influence of heavenly bodies such as excessive heat, cold, rain, &c., &c. ; means and methods have been suggested as to how these pains could be completely avoided, the chief of them being the *acquirement of knowledge of the true nature of all things.* There are many temporary means to avoid the above *pains*, for instance, bodily diseases can be avoided by abstinence and cured by the help of a physician, and so with other pains. But these remedies cannot be procured under all circumstances and at all times and at all places ; besides, there is no guarantee that these pains once removed will not recur.

Figuratively speaking Prakriti (matter) having been married to Prusha (soul) their conjunction produced as a first off-spring the triad of qualities ; each of these qualities which is only known by its effect, has numerous degrees of comparison ; and all the souls below men are believed to be covered with Tama or the quality of darkness of various degrees. It is only in human beings that the three qualities appear successively. It is also a rule that when one of these qualities predominates the other too merge into it ; and they change at every moment like a weather-cock, by the slightest change in circumstances. The effect of *good* or *bad* diet, of *good* or *bad company*, of *good* or *bad thoughts* and *actions* greatly affect these 3 qualities. He who knows well this true nature of the qualities and constantly watches their changes, can by a little *momentary exertion*, always, or for a greater period of time, associate with *sattwa* or tranquility; and thus be in a state to enjoy all the best worldly comforts. In ordinary cases the lowest kind of men such as savages, &c., are believed to be full of Tama or darkness of ignorance; those in the higher grades, *i. e.*, who cultivate their intellectual powers and perform good acts with a view to enjoy their fruits (the worldly pleasures), such as followers of military profession and banking affairs; or who deal with trade, and commerce, with the management of the agricultural population, who administer justice and maintain internal and external orders, &c., are believed to be under the influence of *Rajas* or *activity*; while those *heroic* souls who perform good deeds for goodness sake, who spread morality and piety and are spiritual educators of the people and who themselves are constantly devoted to a study of the *science of life* and the *philosophy of the body and soul*, are replete with *sattwa* or *tranquility*. It is this last class of men, who by continued association with *sattwa* can at last get rid of the influence of these *qualities* and can attain *salvation* or a *complete deliverance* from the *three fold pains of the Sankhya Philosophy*.

THE NYAYA PHILOSOPHY.

The word Nyaya means examining a thing very minutely by breaking it to pieces. The book is compiled by Gautama Rishi and is in fact a good treatise on *Logic.*

There is an allegory of a beautiful description given in an old book, the *Shatapata Brahmin*, in which *night* and *moon* are figuratively related as *wife* and *husband*, because they live together, moon, her ornamental companion, always shining in the night; and as night disappears when the sun rises, so figuratively speaking, it is said that the sun embraces the night, ruins her beauty and chastity and takes her away from her husband, the moon, who grieves and looks *pale* and *lightless* at her separation. Another beauty in the Allegory is that night is called *Ahalya* because she swallows day in her mouth; moon is called *Gautama* on account of rapid motion; and sun with his *ten thousand rays of light* is called Indra, or the king of heavenly stars.

This allegory has been mis-interpreted and converted into an indecent story; namely, that *Ahalya*, the wife of *Rishi Gautama* was seduced by Indra the king of Devtas or Gods, who committed adultery with her and was therefore in a rage cursed by the Rishi to have one thousand *female organs* on his face, which organs were subsequently changed into one thousand eyes. T' regret is that many of our brethren of the West have believed the story to be true and have made mention of it in their serious writings, perhaps to show to the world a black spot in the morality of our antiquarian sages and the compilers of the Darshanas who were in fact the fosterers of Divine Wisdom and the messengers of Holy Truth.

Gautama's philosophy is divided into 5 parts. The first contains 61 Sutras, giving the name and brief description of the 16 topics of this philosophy. The 2nd contains 71 Sutras; the 3rd 78; the 4th 50; and the 5th 25 Sutras.

The book opens by the following aphorism, which contains the 16 topics by the full understanding of which and living a life suitable to that understanding, one can reach the gate of salvation.

प्रमान प्रमेय संशय प्रयोजन दृष्टान्त सिद्धान्तावयवतर्क निर्णय-वाद जल्प वितण्डा हेत्वाभासच्छलजाति निग्रह स्थानानां तत्व ज्ञानान्निः श्रेयसाधिगमः ॥

To begin with 4 *pramanas* or tests are given to distinguish right from wrong. They are as follows :—

1. Pratyaksha or test by senses.
2. Anumana ,, inference.
3. Upamana ,, comparison.
4. Shabda ,, verbal authority.

The sacred wisdom of the Vedas is Divine authority, and the writings of certain Rishis are considered as the authority of the Shastras.

Anumana or inference is made up of 5 parts, *viz* :—(1) Pratijna or proposition, (2) Hetu or reason (3) Udaharana or example (4) Upanaya or application of reason (5) Nigamana or conclusion.

The following example will make them clearly understood. The hill is fiery (proposition) because it smokes (reason) whatever smokes is always firey (example) this hill smokes (application of reason) therefore it is fiery (conclusion).

Anumana is divided into 3 kinds, *viz* :—

(1) "**पूर्ववत्**" where cause suggests the effect, as clouds suggest the rains. (2) "**शेषवत्**" where effect proves the cause, as a child proves the existence of a father. 3 "**सामान्यतोदृष्ट**" in which there may be no relation of cause and effect, but may be a certain point of agreement(**साधर्म्य**) for instance, if one cannot go to another place without *travelling*, no body else can do so without *travelling*.

The 2nd topic is Prameya, , ie things which are to be enquired into or thought over. They are 12 in number. Atma or soul, sarira or body, indrayas or senses, artha or objects of senses, budhi or intellect, manas or the organ of will-power, pravriti or activity (which is divided into 3 kinds kayika, wachika and mansika), Dosha or faults also divided into 3 kinds : raga dwesha and moha ; pratyabhava or transmigration ; phala or fruit ; dukha or pain ; and apavarga or salvation.

The 3rd topic is sanshya or doubt, 4th prayojana or motive, 5th drishtanta or example, 6th siddhanta or established doctrine, 7th avayaya or argument split up into 5 parts, 8th tarka or speculation, 9th nirnaya or distinguishing right from wrong, 10th vada or fair discussion, 11th jalpa or wrangling, 12th vitanda or cavilling, 13th hetvabhasa or fallacious reasoning, 14th chhala or artifice, 15th jati or futile arguments, and 16th nigraha-sthana or bringing the discussion to an end.

With this battery of reason Gautama has proved that the root of all evils lies in ashubha vasna or bad desire created by false notions. Bad desires have the residua of previous actions as their back ground. These residua create pravriti or the three kinds of activity to do a karma, *i. e.*, good or bad action, and thus to be compelled to receive reward or punishment as the fruit of that action by births and re-births ; and though good actions and the enjoyment of their fruits afford certain amount of happiness, yet moksha or eternal bliss can only be had by niskam karmas which leave no residua behind them and therefore leave no chance for births which are in reality the true source of misery. To break the ever lengthening and never ending chain of transmigration, Gautama recommends the suppression of *bad desires* and giving up *false notions.*

THE
VAISHESHIKA PHILOSOPHY.

This philosophy is considered by some to be very similar to or rather a supplement of Nyaya Philosophy. It is compiled by Kanada Rishi. This name is said to have been given to him because he used to live on a very spare diet. The word *vaisheshika* means particulars ; this name is given to the book, because it relates to particulars or categories. They are detailed in the following 4th Sutra or aphorism of chapter 1st:—

धर्म विशेष प्रसूताद् द्रव्यगुण कर्म सामान्य विशेष समवायानां पदार्थानां तत्व ज्ञानान्निः श्रेयसम् ॥

Sense—When man acquires the true knowledge of the following six *padarthas* or *categories*, he achieves *true happiness* (1) *drav* or substance, (2) *gunas* or qualities, (3) *karma* or motion (4) *samanya* or genus, or class, (5) *vishesa* or difference and (6) *samvaya* or casual connection.

This book is divided into 10 parts. The first contains 17 Sutras ; the 2nd 37 ; the 3rd 21 ; the 4th 11 ; the 5th 26 ; the 6th 16 ; the 7th 28 ; the 8th 6 ; the 9th 28 and the 10th 16.

A very beautiful and exhaustive description is given of all the elements and the voluntary and involuntary functions of the body, commencing from the eternally existing *pramanus* or atoms. Soul is described as the 8th and *manas* as the 9th *drav* or substance. The 9 *dravs* are as follows :—

Earth, water, fire, air, ether, time, space, manas, (will-power) and *atma* (soul). Each drav has one or more gunas or qualities assigned to it. The gunas are 24 in number. Earth has the quality of *smell*, water that of *taste* and so on. Great discretion must be exercised to know the "**साधर्म्य**" and "**वैधर्म्य**" relations or point of agreement and point of difference of these Dravs ; for instance, water and earth as *elements* belong to one class, but the one is liquid and the other solid and thus they belong to different classes in this respect.

Atma is considered to be eternal and all-pervading ; but when connected with the body, its influence extends only within the space of the body. All the *mineral*, *vegetable* and *animal kingdoms* have *soul* with one or more *functions* ; but *mankind* have *full* and *complete system* of functions and structures, and has been endowed with gunas or qualities like *buddhi* (intellect) which if rightly used can give a real knowledge of all the objects and thus lead to salvation.

PURVA MIMANSA

OR

KARMA PHILOSOPHY.

It is compiled by *Jaimini* Rishi; and is believed to be an essence of the doctrine of *Karma Canda* as given in the *Vedas.*

It is a big book divided into 12 chapters, and each chapter is again divided into many parts. The 1st and 2nd chapters are divided into 4 parts each, and contain 118 and 139 Sutras respectively; the 3rd chapter is divided into 8 parts and contains 360 Sutras; the 4th and 5th are divided into 4 parts each, and contain 160 and 128 Sutras respectively; the 6th chapter is divided into 8 parts and contains 348 Sutras; the 7th, 8th and 9th chapters are divided into 4 parts each, and contain 100, 139 and 161 Sutras respectively; the 10th chapter is divided into 8 parts and contains 577 Sutras, the 11th and 12th are divided into 4 parts each, and contain 246 and 169 Sutras respectively.

The unequal distribution of happiness and misery in this world is a clear proof that the *just* and *impartial* hand of Providence makes this distribution according to the *Karmas* of each individual; therefore it is very necessary for every one, who wishes to enjoy happiness to do good karmas and abstain from bad ones. Says the Yajur Veda Brahmin :—

यन्मनसा ध्यायति तद्वाचा वदति यद्वाचा वदति तत् कर्मणा
करोति यत् कर्मणा करोति तदभिसंपद्यते ॥

Sense in English :—Men reap the fruit of their actions, which are first thought over in the mind, then spoken of by the mouth and after that brought to action.

Jaimini explains this Karma Philosophy in a very exhaustive way. Briefly speaking karmas are divided into many divisions and sub-divisions, the chief of which are the *nisheda*, *sakam* and *niskam*, *i. e.*, bad actions, good actions and good actions without any worldly motive.

When at the time of doing a karma, *fear*, *shame* or *doubt* arises, it must be considered a bad action and must be abandoned under all circumstances; but it is not an easy task to do so. An old Rishi Jaigishava says that to empty an ocean is easier than to empty the mind of bad desires and actions, *i. e.*, to restrain the mind from bad thoughts and deeds. If no attention is paid to the above inner voice of Providence, producing on the *manas* or the organ of will-power, the impressions of fear, shame, and doubt, the *voice* begins gradually to disappear, and the man becomes totally a slave to the *nisheda karmas* or bad thoughts and deeds; and as it is a law of Providence that every thing in nature has a paramount tendency to reproduce itself, so the residua of nisheda karmas, with *wavering fits* and a *noisy storm of confusion*, in which the above-mentioned feeble inner voice can scarcely be heard, create such an intense desire to reproduce or repeat themselves that it is almost beyond the power of an ordinary man to suppress them. Our Rishis, however, have prescribed certain methods to put a stop to the bad thoughts and deeds, one or two of them are given below :—

(1) To prepare a list of all the *nisheda karmas* which one is accustomed to do, and try to get rid of them one by one. (2) To make up a *Time-table*, keeping the mind and body engaged at all times in good works and in good company, so that no time be left for thinking about or committing bad deeds. (3) To keep in view constantly and particularly at the time of great provocations and unsurmountable temptations, the extremely bad after-consequences of nisheda karmas.

Anyhow *nisheda Karmas* must be abandoned, otherwise no progress can be made in religion, and no happiness gained. Mannu says :—

वेदास्त्यागश्च यज्ञाश्च नियमाश्च तपांसिच।
नविप्रदुष्ट भावस्य सिद्धिं गच्छन्ति कर्हिचित् ॥

Sense in English :—He who has no control over his mind and senses, and is a slave to bad thoughts and deeds, cannot derive any benefit from his knowledge of the *Vedas* and cannot achieve any success whatever, even though he may be rigidly following all religious rites and undergoing the severest sorts of Tapas or austerities.

When at the time of doing a karma no fear, shame or doubt haunts the conscience, and the heart feels a sort of satisfaction and pleasure, it is to be considered a good action.

Great discretion must, however, be exercised to distinguish good actions from bad ones. The following words of *Martin Luther* are worth remembering. "***Where God built a church, there the devil would also build a chapel.........In such sort is the devil always god's ape," Methinks the word "*God*" here, as also in many other writings of the Divine Christians, stands for "*good works* and *good people*," and "*devil* for *the evil*" or the evil works and the evil doers.

All the *yajnas*, commencing from the *Agnihotra* and ending with the *Ashvamedha* are considered as sakam karmas, and full directions for their performance are given by Jaimini. *Yajna* is a technical word meaning certain religious observances performed with the help of Pandits or learned men, for the sake of getting rid of pain, and the attainment of happiness in this world as well as in the next. Five of these yajnas are *maha yajnas*, and are considered as an essential part of every man's *daily duties*. Their detail is given in the Social Reform Series No. 2 "the *sandhiya* Paddhati."

It must always be borne in mind that *truthfulness* and *abstinence* from *anger* and *lust*, are the essential conditions for the successful performance of all yajnas.

Further, it must also be remembered that all the *yajnas* from the *Agnihotra* to *Ashvamedha* are divided into two parts, the *outer* and the *inner*; for instance, the outer Agnihotra or fire sacrifice is to burn certain substances, the main object being to purify the atmosphere; the inner Agnihotra is in fact a part of the *Pranayama* of the yoga philosophy, its main object being to purify the internal vital air of the body. This air is divided into 5 parts, *viz*; (1) *Prana* or respiration, (2) *Vyana* or the air diffused over the whole of the body. (3) *Apana* or the flatus in the lower intestines, (4) *Samana* or the air supporting the digestive organs, and (5) *Udana* or the air supporting the head. Prana should be regulated in the day time, this vital air having a connection with the sun; vyana in the night, it having a connection with the moon; their regular practice keeps perfect health and prolongs life. Apana has its connection with heat, its practice strengthens the speech. Samana has a connection with water, its use strengthens the creative organs of the body and purifies the *manas*, or the organ of will-power. Udana purifies intellect. This *Agnihotra* or proper regulation of the *Vital airs* produces, as a general result, many *Siddhis* or extraordinary powers.

It is with reference to the outer as as well as inner parts of all the yajnas that the Chhandogya upanishad chapter V, Section XXIV says as follows :—

1. He who performs a yajna without knowing its real nature, gets its reward like him who forsaking burning coals pours his *oblations* upon ashes.

2. And he who performs a yajna knowing its nature fully, it enlightens all the faculties of the body and is considered a complete yajna.

3. The sins of him, who knowing well, performs a yajna, are instantaneously burnt, like reed tops when put to fire.

The learned Shankaracharya says that as rubbing, &c., makes transparent substances like mirror clearer and clearer, so does the round of *Sakam Karmas*, commencing from the Agnihotra and ending with the Ashvamedha, make *intellect* clear enough to reflect the Divine Light.

Sakam Karmas are repeatedly done for a considerable length of time, the thought arises in one's mind that however long the period of enjoyment of their fruit may be, it, yet, has an end.

It is at this stage that an intense desire is felt to do such karmas, the fruit of which may be everlasting, and such are the *niskam karmas*, or good actions done without any worldly motive. These niskam karmas when repeatedly done, create and increase the power of vivek or discrimination, by help of which, and by a continued regular practice of the niskam karmas, the *residua* of *nisheda karmas*, *i. e.*, bad desires and false notions are destroyed, and *moksha* or salvation attained.

UTTARA MIMANSA
OR
VEDANTA PHILOSOPHY.

This is the most difficult philosophy, but at the same time it is the essential duty of every man to know it. The true spirit of this philosophy can be acquired only by a constant study of the Vedas, by a constant practice of the yoga and by leading a holy life, having full control over the senses and other faculties, *i. e.*, all the *Knowing faculties*,* the *Reflecting faculties*,† the *Affecting faculties*,‡ &c., must be used very moderately and with full discretion, so that the powers of *attention*, *memory*, *perception* and *conception*, &c., be fully developed, and be able to know *Brahm*, which is considered by *vedanta* to be the source of all reality, nay reality itself, concealed like fire in wood and butter in curd.

The Katha Upanishad says that the knowledge of Brahm is very difficult to obtain; mere *arguing* or a knowledge of the *Vedas* is not sufficient; the *intellect* must be united with the *soul*, which is technically called *Adhyatma yoga*, and the syllable *Om* which is considered by the Upanishad as the substance of all the declarations of the Vedas, must be meditated upon. Again, the Upanishad says in its 2nd valli that the knowledge of Brahm can only be known to him whose senses are in full control, whose intellect is clear and concentrated and who has an *ardent desire* to know Brahm.

---

* Knowing Faculties consist of the faculty of language and the faculty by which external objects as well as their qualities are observed.

† The faculty of *Comparison* which is generally used by the poets and orators, and the faculty of *Reason* which is the noblest gift and the choicest blessing which has been endowed to man; it is generally used by the philosophers and the religionists in tracing *cause* and *effect*.

‡ This faculty is divided into 2 parts the Moral feelings and the Selfish feelings; the former consists of *justice*, *benevolence*, and the latter consists of *hope*, *self esteem*, &c.

The *Kena Upanishad says* that Brahm can only be well understood when known as mere knowledge, and when the idea of intellectual existence disappears and the intellect ceases to work. None should expect to acquire the knowledge of Brahm at once, there being different stages, or practices of the yoga, the chief one being Tapas, by which a truth seeker approaches to a clearer and clearer idea of Brahm.

The *Mandukya Upanishad* describing the four modes of existence, *viz.*, the *wakeful* state, the *contemplative* state, the *slumbering* state and the *essential* state, says that *Brahm* is the *universal spirit* comprehending all things both objects of perception as well as those which perception cannot reach. The syllable *Om* is said to be the verbal representative of Brahm, and its recitation as the means by which Brahm can be known.

It is believed and also proved by all the Upanashads that the happiness derived through the senses is but a drop in the ocean when compared with the happiness derived from the knowledge of Brahm. The happiness gained by Sakam Karmas or good actions has but a limited duration, and the enjoyments of the senses only create a desire to repeat them and weaken and even disorder the senses if there is any excess ; besides, old age and sickness are great obstacles gradually depriving from enjoying the worldly pleasures, and finally *death* puts a stop to all the enjoyments. In short, the pleasures of the senses are but transient and do not last longer than the moment of enjoyment. But man wants an unchangeable happiness, which can only be derived from a being unchangeable himself, and that being is Brahm. The clearer the knowledge of Brahm, the greater is the happiness, and the infinite knowledge of infinite Brahm bestows happiness without bounds. One void of this infinite happiness is also void of the knowledge of Brahm. According to this *test* a very large number of the *vedantists* will be found as void of the true knowledge of Brahm.

There is an old Itihasa or tradition and the above-mentioned Vedantists, and other *speculative divines*, must ponder on it well.

Once upon a time *Narada* went to sage *Sanatkumara* and entreated him to give some instructions, saying.—

तरति शोक मात्मवित चश्नच शोचामि ॥

Sense in English :—

Shruti says that those who possess a knowledge of *atma* are free from pains and afflictions, but I (Narada) though well up in the Vedas, * am yet in grief. Pray relieve me from it. Hearing all this, Sanatkumara replied that the knowledge acquired by Narada was merely *nominal*, and pointed out that far beyond it lay the *true knowledge*. He instructed Narada to practise yoga, and perform Niskam Karmas in order to know the true nature of the *indaryas* (senses), *pranas* (vital airs) *manas*, (will-power), *chitta* (thinking faculty), and *buddhi* (intellect), &c., &c.

By this knowledge of the Indrayas, &c., they come in control and never act contrary to their nature and thus there is no cause left for grief.

He who attains this state of peace of mind can thoroughly understand the spirit of *vedanta* philosophy, and *enjoy* its fruit, the real and permanent happiness.

Vedanta Darshana is compiled by *Badarayana* Rishi or the son of *Badari*. For his profound knowledge and compiling a number of noble religious works he won the title of *Vyasa*, and ever since receiving this title he is generally mentioned by the designation, *Vyasa* Rishi. The illustrious Shankaracharya has written a commentary upon Vedanta Darshana and it is this commentary which is generally studied now-a-days. This philosophy as is evident from its name, Vedanta, which means the end or the last portion of the Veda, is a summing up of the doctrines of the Upanishads.

---

* Narada said that he has read the Rig Veda, the Yajur Veda, the Shama Veda, the Atharva Veda, the Itihasa and Purana, Grammar, rituals, the science of numbers, physics, chronology, logic, polity, technology, the science of spirits, archery, astronomy, the science of antidotes, and the fine arts. Vide Chh Upd, chapter 7th, sec, 1st, para, 2nd,

Mention is made in the beginning of the book that only those are competent to study and can derive benefit from it, who are well up in the following 4 sadhans, *viz : vairag*, *vivek*, *Shatsampatti*, and *Mumukshata*, or dispassion, discrimination, the possession of six particular qualifications, and the desire for salvation respectively. The six qualifications of Shat Sampatti are (1) *Shama* or restraining the mind from desiring objects of senses, (2) *Dama* or restraining the senses from the enjoyment of their respective objects, such as the ear from external sounds, eye from sights, &c., (3) *Titiksha*, or the capacity of bearing hardships, like hunger, thirst, heat, cold, &c., (4) *Uparati* or giving up the pursuit of worldly objects as well as the renunciation of *Karma Kanda*, *i. e.*, ordinary religious ceremonies, (5) *Samadan* or concentration of the mind, and (6) *Shraddha* or full confidence in the *Guru* or religious preceptor and implicit faith in the *Shastras*. This last Sadhan is a most difficult and delicate one; but if the first five Sadhans are well mastered, *Shraddha* shall of itself grow in the mind, and like a kind mother shall protect the disciple from all difficulties and dangers, and lead him to the fountain of knowledge.

Vedanta Darshana is also called *Shariraka Sutra* and is divided into 4 chapters containing 555 Sutras altogether. The whole philosophy is an answer to the querry "what is Brahm"? Brahm is defined as that which is the ultimate cause of the *creation*, *preservation* and *destruction* of all that is. He is Sat Chit Ananda or unchangeable, all-wisdom and all-happiness.

The Katha Upanishad says that from Brahm sprang forth the *ether*, from the ether the *air*, from the air the *fire* or heat and light, from the fire the *water*, from the water the *earth*, from the earth the *herbs*, from herbs *food*, from food *seed*, and from seed *man* and *other animated beings* ; and there is a corresponding change, *i. e.* all animated beings die and are changed into seed, seed into herb and so on. To realize Brahm as the regulator of this eternal process is the primary knowledge of Brahm and unsheaths the covering, *Annamaya kosha*, and the sthula sharira or the outer body becomes free from all diseases, &c. The second knowledge of Brahm is to realize him as the sole regulator of Pranas or vital airs; the 3rd knowledge is to realize Brahm as the regulator of manas or will-power; the 4th knowledge is to realize Brahm as the regulator of *intellect*; the 5th knowledge is to realize Brahm as the regulator and supporter of every thing in the external as well as the internal world. All this knowledge, however, is inferior knowledge but with its help can be gained the superior knowledge of infinite Brahm.

It must be stated here that the word "God" is not an exact and proper appellation for Brahm and this is one of the reasons that our brethren of the West make many mistakes. The following description will give an idea of Brahm. All the functions of the body and mind have their appropriate Devtas to regulate them; here again the word Devtas* which in reality means blind or ignorant and impotent forces working in the system, has also been often wrongly translated as gods. Each Devta of the lower functions though independent in its own sphere, is yet subordinate to all other Deotas of the higher functions, and all the Deotas working harmoniously are subordinate to jivatma or human soul, while all the souls though independent in themselves are subordinate to the laws of Iswara, or Providence, or God of the universe, and Brahm is quite distinct from all of them, though they all have their origin and support from Brahm. It being believed that the whole universe including spiritual and material worlds is sprung up from Brahm, like web from a spider; the material world being like the hairs produced on the body, or vegetables growing from the ground. Says an eminent Orientalist, "** They perceived behind the veil of the body, behind the senses, behind the mind, and behind our reason, another atma or subjective self. That self too was to be discovered by a severe moral and intellectual discipline only and those who wished to find it who wished to know, not themselves, but their self, had to cut far deeper

* Devta has many meanings; it is derived from "Div" which has ten different meanings; the mantras of the vedas are called Devatas; the yajnas are called Devatas; functions of the body are called Devatas; man in general is called Devata; mother, father, teacher, sadhus, and prameswara, are also called Devatas, the 5 senses with manas are also called the six Deva or Devatas.

than the senses or the mind, or the reason, or the ordinary Ego. All these too were mere Devtas, bright Apparition, mere names, yet names meant for something. When that point had been reached then the highest knowledge began to dawn; the self within was drawn towards the highest self, Brahm, it found its true self.** "

Vedanta Philosophy describes three kinds of existences, *viz*:—

(1) *Paramarathika* or true existence which is full of happiness and in which there is nothing but Brahm. (2) *Vyavaharika* or practical existence in which Iswara or Providence with His laws is regulating this universe. (3) *Pratibhasika* or illusory existence, as the existence of a serpent in a rope seen in partial darkness, or of silver in a shining shell, of objects seen in the dreaming state, of water in a mirage, &c. It is the duty of every human being to try to reach or rather realise the first existence, the means for which are no other than to remove the veil of ignorance by the acquirement of true knowledge of the nature of all things by *Shravana*, *Manana*, *Niddhyasan*, and *Sakshatkar*, or the hearing or reading of Shastras, thinking over what has been heard or read, arriving at certainty, and practical realization through profound meditation (asampragyata yoga).

One of the most forcible arguments of this philosophy is presented in the following illustration. For an ordinary man this world is like a dream, when he falls asleep he beholds all things around him as if real, while they are in fact the creation of his brain; when he awakes he knows that whatever he considered as real things in the dream, were only delusions. In like manner, when he is dead, he will come to know that the whole of his life was but a *dream* and the creation of his own brain; but immediately after death he will again be compelled by the Justice of Iswara or Providence, to undergo another birth according to his vasna or predominent desire, to reap the fruit of his good or bad deeds of previous birth. With a *mumukshu* (seeker of salvation), however, the case is different. After acquiring the above mentioned four Sadhans of Vairag, Vivek, Shatsampatti and Mumukshata he seeks the company of a Shrotriya and Brahm-nishtha guru; *i. e.*, one who has understood the deep religious philosophy and realized Brahm. Through his *kripa* and *updesha* or good wishes and instructions, the seeker of salvation by a right and regular use of all the functions of his body and mind, awakens their Devatas, and keeps them under his full control; and enjoying the blessings of this world moderately, he traces his steps onward, under the guidance of his *Guru*, and by the proper and continued performance of *shravana, manana, niddhyasan*, and *sakshatkar*, he makes a full search of the all pervading Brahm in the innermost recesses of his soul and realizes him there. This relization unfolds for him the mystery of the universe, makes him free from all pains and afflictions, from the bondage of the body or of the births and rebirths, and confers on him moksha or eternal bliss.